# DAILY ACTS

READ AND PRAY THROUGH THE BOOK OF ACTS

Unless otherwise identified, Scripture quotations are
from the New King James Version.
Copyright © 1982 by Thomas Nelson, Inc. Used by
permission. All rights reserved.

ISBN 978-0-9840393-0-2

The Foursquare Church
Los Angeles, California
http://foursquare.org

## ABOUT THE FOURSQUARE CHURCH

*Daily Acts* is a compilation of devotionals written by more than 30 leaders from The Foursquare Church. The U.S. Foursquare Church comprises almost 1,800 churches that seek to glorify God and advance His kingdom by proclaiming that Jesus Christ is the Savior, Baptizer, Healer and Soon-Coming King. Founded in 1923 in Los Angeles by Aimee Semple McPherson, The Foursquare Church now has churches and gathering places in 140 countries around the world.

# TABLE OF CONTENTS

**TABLE OF CONTENTS**

# FOREWORD

During my first year as president of The Foursquare Church, I clearly sensed that the Lord was directing our church to embrace and return to the foundational truths that allowed the early church to flourish. Those truths and principles are clearly articulated in the book of Acts—the primer for Spirit-filled church life.

In light of that strong sense of purpose for our church, Foursquare ministers all over our nation pledged to read the entire book of Acts once a month during 2011. Our prayer was that, as leaders immersed them-selves in this book, they would be strengthened and prepared for more effective service, congregations would re-engage as salt and light in their communities, and lost and hurting people would find Jesus Christ.

To keep us more clearly focused corporately, Foursquare Leader Prayer, our weekly e-mail that includes a devotional and prayer points, focused on Acts throughout 2011. Several national and international leaders throughout The Foursquare Church wrote these inspiring, honest and often challenging devotionals. Each one provided clear insights into particular passages of this dynamic New Testament book.

What follows is the collection of those insightful devotionals. Each one appears in its entirety, and I feel sure that you will be blessed as you read the observations of the gifted authors who range from Foursquare central office executives, to local pastors, international missionaries, chaplains and even a Life Pacific College student. We have also included new prayer points that might further challenge you as you read this in a personal devotional time or use it as a small group resource.

May God cause the truths of His Word to stir up in you a renewed commitment to pursue life in the Spirit.

*Glenn C. Burris Jr., president*
*The Foursquare Church*

# ACTS 1

*"WE MUST GET ON OUR KNEES, WE MUST HEAR GOD'S VOICE, WE MUST INVEST IN PEOPLE INTENSIVELY, AND WE MUST SEND THEM OUT IN GOD'S TIMING."*
*—STEVE CECIL*

# ACTS 1: LEARN TO WAIT BEFORE WE GO

BY GLENN BURRIS JR.

Ginger Littleton may not be a household name to most people, but she received quite a bit of press recently. She is the only female member of the Bay City School Board in Panama City, Fla., and on December 14, 2010, she was participating in a routine board meeting. Just before 9 p.m., 56-year-old Clay Duke interrupted the proceedings, drew a gun and ordered everyone out of the room—everyone, that is, except for the male board members.

After Ginger left the room, she quietly returned and slipped up behind the gunman, hitting his gun arm with her purse. While not successful in knocking the gun from Clay's hand, she created quite a stir by returning to put herself in harm's way. Ginger took the initiative, however risky, and her actions were captured on video for the world to see. The most pressing question might be, "Why?"

Motivation is considered the driving force that causes us to act in certain ways. Dr. George Erdman, President of EREN Corporation, suggests there are four major motivations in human behavior:

1. Recognition – an interest in respect, regard, esteem, notoriety or celebrity;

2. Influence – an interest in power, control, competition, independence or order;

3. Profit – an interest in wealth, possessions, acquisitions, income or growth;

4. Internal – an interest in morals, duty, intellect, creativity, philanthropy or honor.

Motivations often get revealed in the crucible of life. Jesus gave His followers clear instructions in Acts 1. He asked them to "wait" (Acts 1:4) before He asked them to "go" (Acts 1:8). The sequencing of those instruc-tions had a way of exposing any hidden agendas. If one of His followers was only interested in the spotlight, the miracles, the crowds, the platform or the adrenaline, then that person would have little interest in waiting.

While the waiting might have thinned out the crowd, it also helped focus the mission and led to compelling motivation for those who faithfully, prayerfully waited.

The book of Acts associates the Holy Spirit with wind and fire, and we need those manifestations in the church today just as much as they did then. Waiting before going allows the wind of the Spirit to blow away any distractions or diversions and allows the fire of the Spirit to purify anything polluted or corrupted.

Waiting helps ensure that we will not be driven by insecurities, fear or greed. In fact, waiting before going means our motivation will be so strong that the instincts of self-preservation and survival take a backseat to the goals of rescuing and helping others. "Greater love has no one than this: to lay down one's life for one's friends," (John 15:13, NIV). May 2011 be our year of rediscovering His call to "wait" and to "go"!

Please join us as we read through the book of Acts each day this year. Today, we are reading through chapter 3, since it's January 3. My prayer is that the Lord will revitalize the journey of the early church in all of us in 2011.

*–Glenn Burris Jr., president of The Foursquare Church.*

**Discussion Points:**

1. What benefits are there for the person who prayerfully waits for a season of time before rushing into a new assignment?

2. Describe a time when waiting on the Holy Spirit resulted in clearing away any distractions or diversions, making the way much more productive and fruitful.

3. In what ways does waiting on God build a healthy passion in the person who is waiting?

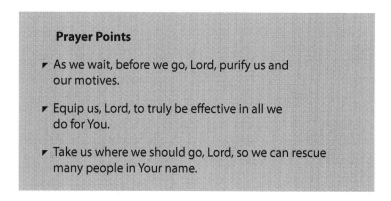

**Prayer Points**

▸ As we wait, before we go, Lord, purify us and our motives.

▸ Equip us, Lord, to truly be effective in all we do for You.

▸ Take us where we should go, Lord, so we can rescue many people in Your name.

# ACTS 1: MAKE THE MOST OF TABLE TALK

BY TAMMY DUNAHOO

Have you ever noticed what happens at the table during a meal with close friends? A relaxed environment creates a place where conversations can go deep quickly.

Jesus knew this, too. We read of a number of significant conversations that took place at the table. For example, He explained the New Covenant around the table during what we have called The Last Supper. At the same meal, Jesus also addressed a betrayer.

Peter was restored by Jesus around the campfire breakfast in John 21; and in many translations and paraphrases, this Acts 1 announcement of the coming Holy Spirit was made during a dinner meal.

An Italian food brand, Barilla, established the project, "Share the Table: The State of Dinnertime in America." In an article on the brand's website, Dr. William Doherty stated: "The dinner table has long been a central meeting place for family and friends to connect. It provides an opportunity to strengthen bonds among family, friends and communities. There is a strong connection between sharing meals and positive life experiences."

The following represents some of the findings from the Barilla project:

1. Americans ranked "connecting with the people who matter most to you" as the most important benefit of sitting down to the table for a meal, with 96 percent of Americans agreeing to this statement.

2. Ninety-six percent of parents with children under 18 in the household agreed that dinnertime gives them an important opportunity to make face-to-face contact with their children, and 92 percent of Americans agreed dinner is one of the few moments in the day where people can

slow down and focus on one another.

3. Americans believe that regular family mealtimes have benefits for children that are less immediately obvious, such as higher performance in school (82 percent agreed), and children who are less likely to abuse drugs and alcohol (80 percent agreed).

Why don't we eat together more often?

1. Adults' work schedules (73 percent)

2. Lack of time (66 percent)

3. Children's schedules (56 percent)

Busy schedules. Lack of time. And, timing. Interestingly, this is the other point Jesus brought to these disciples during the same dinner conversation.

The disciples were concerned about the timing of the restoration of the kingdom. Seems they were pressing Jesus about it with a militant stance. His answer, paraphrased, was this: "You're worried about something that is not your business. Wait, stay together, and receive the Holy Spirit." The fullness of the Holy Spirit was the means by which Jesus would be with them always.

Slow down, and take time for meals with family and friends. God might be saying something life-transforming during dinner!

*–Tammy Dunahoo, Foursquare vice president and general supervisor.*

**Discussion Points:**

1. Share a personal memory you have about the value of a conversation with a trusted friend over a meal.

2. In what ways has the Holy Spirit spoken to you during times of fellowship with others?

3. What would it take for you to slow down enough to enjoy some healthy table talk?

**Prayer Points**

▸ God, I need Your help to slow down and spend time in deep conversation with others.

▸ Show me the simple, yet profound, value of sharing time with others over a meal.

▸ Speak clearly through my friends and family so that I can be refreshed and prepared to serve You.

# ACTS 1: HEARING GOD; SENDING PEOPLE

BY STEVE CECIL

After Judas had betrayed Jesus and took his own life, the disciples were determined to replace him with someone. I'm not sure if twelve was a magical number that they wanted to stick with for some reason, but for whatever reason they decided to add someone. Somehow they made up a criteria, dwindled it down to a couple of people they deemed ready and basically played an ancient version of "rock, paper, scissors" for it. (Interestingly, this is the last time the drawing of lots is mentioned in the Bible. Could the pouring out of the Spirit on Pentecost have something to do with that?)

I've often thought, "Good thing Jesus didn't select the original twelve like this." If he had, I'm not really sure that any of them would have made the cut. I'm sure that Peter himself wouldn't have fit their criteria.

The model Jesus gives us is quite different. Jesus prayed all night and God showed Him whom he should choose to be on the team. And because of this, Jesus got the right people.

How often do we choose people based on human determination? We look at all the qualifications, we do the interviews, we talk about who would be the best fit and then we place people in the positions for which we think they are qualified.

I'm not saying we should throw away a grid that helps us determine where people fit based on their gifting, character and passion. What I would argue is that this better not be the only method we use, and it should certainly never be the final word. God's voice should be.

How many Peters, Pauls and Johns would not even be on our radar if we only used human methods of deciding who should be on the team? The hard work we are called to is hearing the voice of God, potentially choosing people who are pre-qualified and investing in them until they are ready to be sent out.

Think about this: in both the "choosing of someone to be on the team" and the "sending them out," it is utterly important to hear the voice of God.

Because again, I'm sure the disciples didn't feel ready for Jesus to leave and to be left in charge of the ministry, but Jesus knew it was the right time. And often, left to our own determination, we decide that people aren't ready to be sent out.

The bottom line is that we desperately need more people on the team. This truth makes me think that maybe the disciples wanted twelve because they knew that they needed more people on the team, too. Knowing this, we have to ask ourselves: what are going to be the determining factors in discovering and sending these new leaders?

The answer: we must get on our knees, we must hear God's voice, we must invest in people intensively, and we must send them out in God's timing.

*–Steve Cecil, NextGen/Young Adults and Rising Leaders facilitator for the Heartland District and co-pastor of The Journey (Madison-Metro Foursquare Church) with his wife, Kim.*

### Discussion Points:

1. When you think about Jesus' disciples and their particular qualities, with which one do you personally identify, and what characteristics do you share in common?

2. How do you think God selects the right people to become His messengers?

3. What steps should we take to ensure that we train and send the people God has called for the task?

**Prayer Points**

▸ Help me hear You clearly above all the other voices that vie for attention.

▸ Especially when I'm looking for the right team players, please guide my decision-making.

▸ Sensitize my eyes and ears so that I encourage the right people serving in the right places.

# ACTS 2

*"WHILE IT MAY BE TRUE THAT THE CHURCH HAS EXERCISED ITS MINISTRY IN THE POWER OF HUMAN STRENGTH AND WIT, THE HOLY SPIRIT IN EVERY GENERATION IS FAITHFUL TO BRING THE CHURCH BACK TO THE REALITY THAT BEING WITNESSES FOR CHRIST IS IMPOSSIBLE WITHOUT THE POWER OF THE HOLY SPIRIT."*

*—MICHAEL MCGOVERN*

# ACTS 2: RELYING ON THE HOLY SPIRIT MORE THAN PEOPLE

BY MICHAEL MCGOVERN

The Foursquare tribe is being encouraged by our leaders to make the book of Acts the focal point of our family for 2011. The "lot" has fallen to me to draw my devotion this week from Acts, chapter two.

Initially, I thought surely Harold Helms or Jack Hayford should have been given this assignment, but then again, "For the promise is to you and to your children, and to all who are afar off, as many as the Lord our God will call," (Acts 2:39, NKJV). At one time, everybody is "far off," even Harold and Jack.

None of us miss the importance of the day recorded in Acts 2:1, when "Pentecost had fully come." Acts 2 has been considered the Pentecostal Primer for 2,000 years. The faithful Jew had been celebrating this feast since the time of Moses, but at this Pentecost, God would break in on their traditional yearly observance with a new thing, and the first fruits of Holy Spirit-empowered believers began to emerge.

None of those in the upper room—or any of us—would dare say that mere man could accomplish the task of making disciples of all nations. Yet that has been the on-again-off-again approach of the church for two millennia.

In their book, *Tragedy in the Church: The Missing Gifts*, A.W. Tozer and editor Gerald B. Smith observe:

"A Christian congregation can survive and often appear to prosper in the community by the exercise of human talent and without any touch from the Holy Spirit! All that religious activity and the dear people will not know anything better until the great and terrible day when our self-employed talents are burned with fire and only that which was wrought by the Holy Ghost will stand forever!"

Tozer also writes: "in most Christian churches the Spirit is quite entirely overlooked. Whether He is present or absent makes no real difference to anyone" (*Tozer on the Holy Spirit: A 366-Day Devotional*). I suspect this is a sad commentary on ministry in general in Western Europe and North America.

While it may be true that the church has exercised its ministry in the power of human strength and wit, the Holy Spirit in every generation is faithful to bring the church back to the reality that being witnesses for Christ (see Acts 1:8) is impossible without the power of the Holy Spirit.

Not only will our gospel witness be fruitless without His power, it also will not be fruitful if not aligned with the Word of God! There is a timeless truth from the mouth of the apostle Peter when he said: "But this is what was spoken by the prophet Joel: 'And it shall come to pass in the last days, says God, that I will pour out of My Spirit on all flesh; Your sons and your daughters shall prophesy, young men shall see visions, your old men shall dream dreams,'" (Acts 2:16-17, NKJV).

The earliest moments of Spirit-empowered ministry took its lead from Scripture. That which was, should be that which still is! I pray that focusing on the book of Acts in 2011 will result in another level of renewal for all of us by His Word and His Spirit.

*–Michael McGovern, supervisor of the Great Northern District.*

### Discussion Points:

1. In what ways has the Holy Spirit broken in on your beliefs, traditions, and religious practices?

2. Describe your response to this statement: "In most Christian churches, the Spirit is quite entirely overlooked. Whether He is present or absent makes no real difference to anyone," (*A. W. Tozer on the Holy Spirit: A 366-Day Devotional*).

3. How will you be more open to the working of the Holy Spirit in your life and ministry? Be specific.

### Prayer Points

▸ Make us passionate, Lord, for the presence of Your Holy Spirit.

▸ Remind us daily of our need for Your presence and power.

▸ Fill us, Holy Spirit, that we will be able to do everything You have in mind for us.

# ACTS 2: GO REACH THE NATIONS FOR GOD

BY JERRY STOTT

It is 5 a.m., and I'm off to the airport to speak at a youth outreach in the northern area of Indonesia. I am full of expectation about what the Holy Spirit will do, and I believe it will look like something straight out of Acts 2. Let me share with you why I have such high expectations.

Last Wednesday, I was speaking to a group of 1,000 Christian Indonesians between the ages of 11 and 16. We were in a community largely populated with Muslims, and I could see seven different mosques from the front door of my hotel.

At the end of the teaching, I asked these young people how many of them had been filled with the Holy Spirit and were living with God's power on a daily basis.

Only a handful responded affirmatively. I was shocked.

When I invited them to the altar for prayer to be filled with the Holy Spirit, hundreds of them came forward! In front of my eyes, nearly 1,000 young ones received the baptism with the Holy Spirit with the evidence of speaking with other tongues.

It seemed to me to be something that you would only read about from Azusa Street or the early days of Angelus Temple. The Holy Spirit swept over the whole place, and these young people just started dropping everywhere and praying in the Spirit.

In my life I've seen just about every kind of miracle, but watching the Lord touch these precious Indonesian young people with His love and power has to be a new high point for me.

After experiencing this incredible occasion, I reflected again on Acts 2:1-6. I realized anew that to be filled with the Holy Spirit is to be full of God to reach others.

The Lord reminded me that the Holy Spirit gives power to the church when we come together in unity, in prayer and with a common hunger for the Lord. God fills people who expect His touch, and then He uses those people to spread His touch to others.

The promise of Acts 1:8 is that we will receive power that will enable us to reach people from the very ends of the earth. The power that was released on that historic Day of Pentecost was not just for those believers. They were given power in order to win the lost from all nations. And they did.

Wherever the Holy Spirit is pouring out His power—in Jerusalem or Indonesia or maybe even in your town—He intends for His power to equip us to win people everywhere, in every language and nation, to Him.

Allow your hunger for the Lord to move you to be filled with the Holy Spirit. Then go. Reach the nations for God.

*—Jerry Stott, Foursquare South Pacific area missionary.*

### Discussion Points:

1. How would you describe your hunger for God? For His miracles? For His presence?

2. What would happen in your ministry if the Holy Spirit showed up in the fullness of His power?

3. How full do we need to be with the Holy Spirit to be equipped to reach the nations for God?

### Prayer Points

▸ Holy Spirit, fill me with Your fullness and Your power.

▸ Equip me to share Your presence with others.

▸ Allow revival to come through the obedience of Your people.

# ACTS 2: FINDING GOD

BY TIM CLARK

Question: "Where is God?" Pastor and author Jerry Cook repeatedly asks this question to congregations. Hearing him ask it recently in a college chapel service made me start to think. Deists are content to leave God in heaven. He's "up there" somewhere, but probably unconcerned with what's happening on earth.

Humanists freeze Jesus on earth. They think we should remember the nice things He did and said when He was here. He's a really good man to follow, they say, but not much more than that.

Some Catholic and Orthodox believers keep Jesus on the cross. What a wonderful reality that He died for our sins, and we'd have no place in God's family if it weren't for the cross. I preach about the cross every Sunday. But that's not where we find God now.

Many evangelical Christians live with a constant focus on the resurrection and ascension. Jesus is alive! He's back in heaven with the Father, building us a home. Mansions and feasts are waiting for us in the sweet by-and-by, in the sky, when we die.

But none of that really answers the question, does it? Where is God?

He's right here! At Pentecost the Father and the Son sent the Holy Spirit to dwell in and through His people. In Col. 1:27, Paul puts it this way: "Christ in you, the hope of Glory." In Corinthians we find all believers are given the One Spirit to dwell in us.

Though He is manifest in these places, we don't just find God in the cosmos, among creation, on the cross, or in some celestial future home—we discover that God is fully present and active in the daily lives of those who have been reborn by and filled with His Spirit.

And that is the point of Acts 2:42-47; it's not so much a model given for us to follow as it is an exciting account of what spontaneously started to happen when 3,000 people were radically transformed by the Spirit. When God lives in you, you can't help responding in ways that reflect God.

Too often we take the book of Acts and try to build a structure and strategy that will help us to look like the early church. Instead, let's wholly engage the wonder that God lives in us, and then fully participate in whatever happens as a result of that awesome reality.

*–Tim Clark, district supervisor of the Greater Los Angeles District.*

### Discussion Points:

1. What beliefs about God have influenced your life?
2. Describe a circumstance in your life when you struggled to find God.
3. What does the phrase "Christ in you, the hope of glory" mean in your life today?

### Prayer Points

▸ Please show Yourself powerful in my life so I know with certainty that You are with me.

▸ As I seek You, Lord, soften my heart so I will find You.

▸ Accomplish through my life greater things than the first-century Christians experienced!

# ACTS 3

*"WE HAVE THE MESSAGE THAT THE WORLD IS DYING TO HEAR. GOD IS SAYING TO EACH OF US THAT WE NEED TO BREAK OUT OF OUR CHURCHES, NOTICE THESE PEOPLE, AND TELL THEM ABOUT HIM."*
*—DEAN TRUETT*

# ACTS 3: BELIEVING IN WHAT I HAVE

BY TAMMY DUNAHOO

It's a divine setup: a beggar at the right place, at the right time, needing a miracle, but only asking for alms. Then, the disciples arrive, at the right place, at the right time, having no alms, but possessing a miracle.

This encounter found in Acts 3 causes me to look at myself and ask if I would have had the same quick response as the disciples. There's nothing inferred in the text that makes us think they checked their pockets or collaborated about what they should do. Rather, the need brought about an immediate reply; one of those "out of the abundance of the heart his mouth speaks" (Luke 6:45, NKJV) types of answers. It's a response that says, "Then Peter said, '…what I do have I give you: In the name of Jesus Christ of Nazareth, rise up and walk,'" (Acts 3:6).

Every day we encounter broken humanity, people with no ability to heal themselves, who are often even asking the wrong questions. In response, I wonder if I'm sometimes too busy to recognize the divine setup that has come across my path. How often do I walk by, dropping in some change, apologizing that I don't have more to give, or maybe even walk by pretending to not see the person?

I've learned that my beliefs are the real motivators of my behaviors, but when I read Acts 3, I have to question how deeply I believe in "what I have."

When I was a little girl, my grandfather was on the board of directors for the Kathryn Kuhlman Ministry. I will never forget the first time I saw her in the Shrine Auditorium in Los Angeles. With her unique voice and pronunciation she proclaimed, "I believe in miracles!" The "r's" when she said "miracles" seemed to roll off her tongue in a way that mesmerized my young attention span. I couldn't take my eyes off her, and yet it was more than her voice. She believed so deeply and communicated that belief in such a way that the supernatural seemed incredibly natural. Her belief in "what she had" caused people to respond and say, "Well, of course!"

The first week of December, Gary and I visited New York City for a few days of fun. As we walked through Macy's department store, the word "Believe" was everywhere, including in huge lights on the front of the store. The windows were dressed with the classic Christmas story *Miracle on 34th Street*. I found myself caught up in the childlikeness of it all, and I was reminded how people everywhere truly long to believe in the miraculous.

So I have to ask myself these questions: When I respond to human need with only human supply, what do I really believe? When I encounter seemingly huge issues, do I depend on His miracle-abundance, even though I may have a mere five loaves and two fish? I must ask these questions to identify my self-reliant behavior. I must ask so I can identify the comfortable places where I give away tangible "things" that I have without taking a risk to truly believe for what God has in mind.

Should we give the practical? Absolutely! But the practical without the miraculous will not transform a life. We must give the cup of cold water, feed the poor, give shelter to the homeless, all in the name of Jesus, believing that the same power that raised Christ from the dead dwells in us.

Five loaves and two fish become more than enough to answer the need of multitudes. Spirit-empowered statements cause beggars to walk and leap and praise God. A cup of cold water becomes refreshment for the soul, bread becomes life to the spirit, and a home becomes an eternal future for the homeless.

Our daily pathways are not coincidental but providential. Believe!

*–Tammy Dunahoo, Foursquare vice president and general supervisor.*

### Discussion Points:

1. How deeply do you really "believe in what you have" in Christ?

2. Describe a time when your belief broke through the circumstances of life and really made a difference for someone.

3. In what ways have you depended on God's miracle-abundance, even though all you could see were a mere five loaves and two fish?

### Prayer Points

➤ Thank you, Lord, for equipping me with Your presence.

➤ Help me remember that Your power in my life is all I need to do great things for Your kingdom.

➤ Give me boldness to speak Your Word and live in your authority daily.

# ACTS 3: IF I DON'T TELL THEM, WHO WILL?

BY DEAN TRUETT

For 10 years, my wife, Carlene, and I traveled all over Latin America as Foursquare missionaries-at-large. On one of our trips to a large coastal city in Colombia, a man asked to speak with me. "My pastor says that I should not do what I am doing," he began. "I want to know what you think."

The man described how he left the city every other weekend to minister to guerilla soldiers in the mountain regions of Colombia. He said that every other Saturday he would travel by bus for two hours, and would get off the bus in the middle of nowhere and simply wait under a tree.

Sometimes he waited for only 10 minutes, and other times an hour, but eventually the soldiers came out of the mountains to get him and take him back to their camp. From Saturday until Sunday afternoon, he would sit with different groups of between 10 and 12 men, and talk to them about the Lord Jesus Christ.

At noon on Sunday, they would take the man to the highway, and he would catch a bus back to town. He was aware that at any moment the guerilla soldiers could kill him, and no one would ever know what happened to him.

What many people did not know is that most of these "men" were actually boys, between just 12 and 14 years of age.

As he finished telling me his story, the man looked at me and said, "Pastor Dean, if I don't tell them, who will?"

In Acts 3, we find Peter entering the temple, where he has an encounter with a beggar. We have no way of knowing how many times Peter had passed the same man on his way into the temple; surely they crossed paths many times, and it seems Peter had never noticed him. This time was different. This time, God opened Peter's eyes to see the need of the man.

Peter told the man that he did not have money; instead, he had something better: " 'In the name of Jesus Christ of Nazareth, rise up and walk.' And he took him by the right hand and lifted him up, and immediately his feet and ankles received strength. So he, leaping up, stood and walked and entered the temple with them—walking, leaping and praising God" (Acts 3:6-9, NKJV).

The world we live in today is lost and hurting. Every day we walk by dying people and, too often, we don't see them or their needs. We have the message that the world is dying to hear. God is saying to each of us that we need to break out of our churches, notice these people, and tell them about Him.

That man in Colombia said it best: "If I don't tell them, who will?"

*–Dean Truett, retired Foursquare missionary and active prison chaplain.*

### Discussion Points:

1. What advice would you have given the man in Colombia? His pastor thought his behavior was too risky.

2. Who is that person in your life—someone you see every day who needs the love of God—with whom you've not yet taken the time to speak?

3. In what ways can you "break out of your church" and share the gospel with the world?

### Prayer Points:

- ► Lord, open our eyes that we might see the needs of others.

- ► Help me break out of my comfort zone and share Jesus' love with the world.

- ► Stir my heart, that I might be willing to go wherever You tell me, Lord.

# ACTS 3: MORE MONEY ISN'T ALWAYS THE ANSWER

BY JOHN FEHLEN

In Acts 3 we find an important reminder of how we should approach life and ministry.

Peter and John were confronted by a beggar near the entrance to the temple, and he was looking for money. It is unknown whether or not they would have given him money if they had some. I don't think it's inherently wrong to give out money to those in need; nor is the text making that point. However, Peter and John had no money, so they said, "Silver and gold we don't have, but what we do have we will give."

They had Jesus. So they gave him Jesus.

How often do we rely upon money as the answer to most, if not all, things? Are we too quick to throw dollars at something rather than apply the message and ministry of Jesus? In our culture, even within the local church, we have a default propensity toward money as The Answer. Have we perhaps overlooked and/or minimized Jesus? He is the only one who causes a paralyzed man to instantly rise up and begin to walk, leap and worship. That's something that money really can't buy.

I wonder if our ongoing economic realities have forced us to lean harder upon Jesus. When there isn't much in terms of silver and gold, then we must go to Jesus. But what happens then, when the silver and gold starts to flow again? Is Jesus put on the back burner? Let's make sure that doesn't happen.

*–John Fehlen, pastor of West Salem Foursquare Church in Oregon.*

### Discussion Points:

1. How can money interfere with life and ministry?

2. In what ways does God equip us to minister even when money is scarce?

3. What do you think the paralyzed man learned about God because of what Peter and John said to him and the miracle that resulted?

### Prayer Points:

- Lord, help me to be very generous with everything You've given me.

- When I wish for more—money, resources, stuff— convict me that what I really need is more of You.

- Don't let me drift away from You during times of plenty; keep me close even when I have enough.

# ACTS 4

*"GOD SEES VALUE AND POTENTIAL IN PEOPLE NOT BECAUSE OF THEIR NATURAL GIFTING, ABILITIES OR COMPETENCIES, BUT BECAUSE HE SEES WHAT WE CAN BE WHEN WE'RE CALLED BY HIS NAME, FILLED WITH THE HOLY SPIRIT..."*
**—LOUIE D. LOCKE**

# ACTS 4: PERSIST WHEN OTHERS GIVE UP

BY GEORGE BUTRON

Paul (not his real name) leads a ministry in a nation known for corruption, oppression and paranoid leadership. The growth is like something out of the book of Acts, and the persecution could come right out of Acts 4.

He was arrested and held by the police for two weeks, while he slept on a cement floor. The Bible college he had started was closed, and he was accused of being a subversive. He was beaten with an iron bar, and the injuries he suffered were so severe, he required surgery as a result.

The authorities knew Paul had done nothing wrong, but they were looking for a payoff to secure his release from prison. The money was raised, and the transaction made for his freedom. During all of this, I never heard him complain and never saw bitterness or resentment in his attitude. He never faltered in ministry or considered leaving his nation, though many leaders of his caliber have emigrated to less-threatening places.

Instead, he has carried on with his work and secured new land to build a new Bible college that today trains 36 students. In spite of the constant threat, Paul has planted 90 churches in all, with 16 new churches planted and 1,000 people baptized in 2010.

He does not have a dominant or outspoken personality but does have a quiet and consistent determination. He persists when others would give up—and Paul is a man of persistent prayer. Through his amazing and challenging experiences, he is known among the leaders and churches he oversees as a leader with a spirit of prayer and dependency on God.

In the midst of such difficult circumstances, believers have given possessions and sold properties to advance the ministry and care for one another. Last year, through sacrificial giving, a new church headquarters building was dedicated that will seat 1,000 people. At present, the government has just announced that they are taxing this new building $19,000 USD, and the first payment is due immediately. Paul has no money and already sold land last year to pay a similar tax on the new Bible college. To make matters worse, his motorcycle was stolen just before Christmas.

What will he do? The same thing believers did in the first century, and have always done when facing impossible situations: Paul will persist when others give up! I consider it a high honor to be able to serve with believers like Paul who are living out the book of Acts today.

–*George Butron, Foursquare Southeast Asia area missionary*.

### Discussion Points:

1. What does it take for a person to live in complete dependence on God, even when others give up?

2. How persistent are you as a man or woman of prayer?

3. Describe an experience you have had when you persisted in prayer and saw God bring deliverance.

### Prayer Points

► Remind me daily, Lord, that You are the source of anything I need

► As You provide for my needs, help me respond with gratitude and joy.

► Equip me to persevere in Your strength, especially when those around me give up.

# ACTS 4: GOING VIRAL IN JESUS' NAME

BY BONITA SANCHEZ

If the Internet had been available during the time of Peter and John, they might have been captured on video and put on YouTube when they spoke to the crippled man and told him to get up and walk (see Acts 4:8-10). And it wouldn't have made the religious leaders of the day very happy.

This crippled man was well-known because he sat at the entrance of the temple every day, begging. In exchange for doing good to this man, the religious leaders put Peter and John in jail overnight. The following morning when the elders and teachers of the law gathered, Peter and John were questioned: " 'By what power or what name have you done this?'" (v. 7, NKJV).

Peter pointed out the irony that the leaders were upset because a man had been healed, and he wondered why they were so angry about such an act of kindness. He also pointed out that the man had been healed in the name of Jesus, whom these leaders had crucified.

Peter and John were caught doing a good thing for someone, and even without the benefit of YouTube, their act of kindness went "viral."

As I read again the story of Peter and John from Acts 4, I was reminded of a global project started by Phillip Cotsford in August 2010 called "Caught Doin' Good." He is a young man who is traveling the world trying to catch people in the act of being kind to others.

Schoolteachers have used the idea as a motivational tool for teaching children to do right. Companies have also grasped this idea and are producing pencils, coins, bracelets and certificates with this slogan.

Peter and John were in trouble with the leaders because they caught them in the act of doing a good deed for someone. The leaders saw the evidence before their own eyes: the crippled man stood among them and walked. There was no denying it; the disciples used the powerful name of Jesus, and everyone saw the miraculous results.

What about us? Who is watching us today? Are they observing miraculous works of God being done in and through us? Are we looking for others whom we can catch in the act of doing good things in the name of Jesus?

*–Bonita Sanchez, a Foursquare missionary in Panama with her husband, Gino.*

**Discussion Points:**

1. In what ways are you allowing God to use you to do the miraculous?

2. How do you recognize and encourage the expectation of others that God will do miracles in your church?

3. What is the response from your community when genuine miracles happen?

**Prayer Points:**

➤ Help me notice the good that others are doing around me in Jesus' name.

➤ Show me, Lord, who is watching my life, that I might truly be Your witness.

➤ Use me to bring Your healing and wholeness to hurting and dying people.

# ACTS 4: NORMAL PEOPLE FOLLOWING JESUS

BY LOUIE D. LOCKE

How our world and culture measure value, potential and "special-ness" in people is largely based on brains, brawn, looks and special abilities. This type of thinking and evaluating can find its way into the church as well—it can sound a little like this: "That person is so gifted and talented! If they became a Christian, God could really do big things through them."

Sound familiar?

By the time Jesus had chosen the disciples, they each had most likely been passed over as "not good enough" by local rabbis seek-ing out promising young disciples. Sure, they'd all been taught the Torah, God's law, and the prophets when they were children, but as they grew up, each one learned a trade or joined the family business.

And then Jesus called them to "follow Me" (Matt. 4:19).

The disciples were chosen not because of their greatness or special abilities—Jesus chose them because they were normal. They were common, regular people with nothing really remarkable about them.

God sees value and potential in people not because of their natural gifting, abilities or competencies, but because He sees what we can be when we're called by His name, filled with the Holy Spirit: "… Christ in you, the hope of glory," (Col. 1:27).

It's important to keep this in mind when we evaluate our own and others' fitness and abilities to be used by the Lord. Too often we disqualify ourselves for God's use based upon our shortcomings, weaknesses, struggles and inadequacies, as though God didn't know these things about us when He called us.

It's vital for us to remember that what really matters is being with Jesus. It is impossible to be with Him and not be forever changed.

May the same things that were said of Peter and John be said about us—that it is Christ in us that makes us special.

*–Louie D. Locke, senior pastor of Fountainhead Foursquare Church in Carson City, Nev.*

### Discussion Points:

1. What personal characteristics do you think are highly desired in the kingdom of God? By people? By God?

2. Describe a time when you may have felt undesired or unwelcome in the body of Christ?

3. How can we make a place for common, regular people in Christian service today?

### Prayer Points:

▸ Thank you, God, for choosing me to be one of Your followers.

▸ As I learn to love You more, encourage my heart that I am qualified to be Your servant.

▸ Refresh my memory regularly as I realize that it's You in me that makes me special.

# ACTS 5

*"THE LAST THING I WANT TO BE SAID OF
MY LIFE IS THAT I OPPOSED GOD."*
**—JOHN FEHLEN**

# ACTS 5: NEVER FORGET THAT GOD IS AWESOME

BY KIM CECIL

"Acts 5?" my husband, Steve, inquired in an amused tone. "That's the one with Ananias and Sapphira! Good luck." I was deeply honored to be asked to share my thoughts on the book of Acts, but I also shared Steve's opinion that this would be a difficult story to tackle.

The truth is, the chronicle of Ananias and Sapphira messes with our concept of grace. Of redemption. Of God covering our mistakes. We think we have it all together, a nice gospel package with no loose ends. Then we read this story and think: "What am I supposed to do with this?" It's not easily preachable, is it? And yet it is in there, in the precious Word of God, and we only do ourselves discredit if we don't tackle it intellectually and spiritually.

God is not predictable. Although His character never alters—He is love unconditional and grace undeserved—the way He moves in and through humanity cannot easily be calculated or mapped. He is an "awesome God," as the psalmists of old and modern-day psalmist Rich Mullins have said. In his famous song "Awesome God," Mullins sings: "Judgment and wrath He poured out on Sodom; mercy and grace He gave us at the cross. I hope we have not too quickly forgotten that our God is an awesome God."

What do I personally take away from the story of Ananias and Sapphira, and what lesson can be gleaned for the body of Christ as a whole? Without coming to any clear theological conclusions on why God chose to judge the couple in this way, it seems fairly clear that I should maintain inner and outer integrity with the Lord and with others.

"You have not lied to men but to God," Peter tells Ananias in Acts 5:4 (NKJV), and that alone is a clarion call for me to uphold an honesty in my heart toward the Lord that can only be considered ruthless. No hiding from God my true motives and struggles; no manipulation or flattery will be accepted.

The same holds true for the body of Christ. We do ourselves a great disservice when we allow insecurities and fear of what others will think to rule our behaviors, instead of being honest about our personal walk with Christ and our struggles as we go. If God knows everything anyway, why hide it?

This is a tough story with tough lessons that ultimately we learn along with the early church. "I hope we have not too quickly forgotten that our God is an awesome God."

*–Kim Cecil, Heartland District missions representative and co-pastor of The Journey (Madison-Metro Foursquare Church) with her husband, Steve.*

### Discussion Points:

1. How does a person maintain "internal and external" integrity?

2. What does "ruthless honesty" with God look like in your life?

3. Imagine aloud for a moment what awesome things God wants to do for you and for your city.

**Prayer Points**

- Lord, help me to be completely transparent and honest with You.

- Keep showing me just how awesome You are every day of my life.

- Remind me regularly how much You want to do in me to touch the world.

# ACTS 5: BLIND, YET THINKING WE SEE

BY JIM SCOTT

It's frustrating, sometimes embarrassing, amusing and disconcerting being partially red-green-brown color-blind.

It's frustrating, because every day is a challenge when I get dressed. Melinda must be with me when I buy clothes. ("The slacks and jacket look fine together—honest!") It's embarrassing, because I'm wrong more than I'm right when I point out something to a friend using color. ("That shirt is purple, not blue.") And it's amusing, because I become a point of interest when someone learns I'm color-blind. ("What color does this look like to you?" "What color is that car?")

But my color-blindness is also disconcerting. I believe I can see, but I'm blind to what is true and real. In fact, I only know I'm color-blind because others continue to confirm it. I cannot see certain colors even though I know I'm blind to those colors. I live every day knowing I'm missing so much because something is broken in my eyes.

My daily experiences with this mild form of blindness connected with Acts 5:12-40 in a way that startled me. In the first portion of the text, we read that the apostles performed many miraculous signs, wonders, healings and deliverances. These miracles were so extraordinary that people in Jerusalem and the surrounding area were both repelled and compelled.

Still, people believed, and the congregation grew.

The second and larger portion of the text describes time in jail for the apostles, a miraculous release from jail, instructions by an angel of the Lord, their second arrest, court proceedings, questioning, judgment and flogging of these same apostles. Is this any way to treat people who do signs and wonders, who heal the sick and cast out demons?

I doubt if the high priest and his associates realized the apostles were doing these miracles. It is probable that the high priest and his associates were blinded and could not see these miracles. We read in Acts 5:17, 28 and 33 that these leaders were "filled with jealousy," afraid that they would be blamed for Jesus' death, and they were "furious" with the apostles.

Jealousy, fear and rage are powerful, and they can impact how a person "sees."

This passage reminded me of Peter's reaction during the arrest of Jesus. As Jesus was confronted, and in the fear and confusion of the moment, "One of them struck the servant of the high priest and cut off his right ear. But Jesus answered and said, 'Permit even this.' And He touched his ear and healed him" (Luke 22:50-51, NIV).

Please forgive this graphic description, but it serves the larger point. A portion of the ear may be on the ground, the blood still wet on the servant's head and shoulder. But now, he has a new ear. The servant is healed before all their eyes in verse 51, and Jesus is seized and taken away in verse 54.

Hatred and fear blinded these men.

The lessons here are significant for me. Among them is the humility to recognize what I think I "see" and "know." Also important is my quick repentance and confession when I find sin and frailty in me, so that my sight is not hindered. This recognition is followed by a request to the God who loves me that He will daily help me see accurately.

By the way, it will be so amazing to see all the colors in heaven!

*–Jim Scott, vice president of Global Operations / director of Foursquare Missions International.*

### Discussion Points:

1. Describe a time when you realized your physical sight wasn't quite what you thought it was. What happened, and what was the result?

2. Now do the same for an experience with spiritual sight.

3. Have you identified any weakness or personal flaw that keeps you from seeing the full expression of the Holy Spirit in your church? If so, what will you do to change that?

**Prayer Points:**

➤ Even when I think I see, Lord, show me what You see.

➤ Forgive me of my sin, that my spiritual sight will not be hindered.

➤ Remind me to be thankful for Your constant and careful watch over my life.

# ACTS 5: GETTING IT RIGHT, LIKE GAMALIEL

BY JOHN FEHLEN

You know, sometimes even a Pharisee gets it right.

Throughout the gospels the ruling class of leaders and teachers of the law are always getting slammed. Every time you turn around the Pharisees are taking it in the teeth. Jesus would often single them out for their internal contamination, and the Apostle Paul, having been in their camp at one time, would call them on the carpet. It seems like they couldn't get a break … until now.

Gamaliel.

Gamaliel was a teacher of the law who was held in great esteem by the people of that time. He spoke some profound things in Acts 5 that the body of Christ ought to consider. In response to the activities of Peter and the apostles, and their subsequent arrest, Gamaliel issued a caution: if God is at work, then watch out, and if He is not then it will crumble.

In the years that I have been a part of the church, and more specifically as a pastor of a local church, I have seen a number of "movements" surface and gain momentum. Some have been loopy, some downright heretical and others just different from what I am accustomed. Admittedly, I have occasionally been far too quick to decry them and label them as not of God. Maybe I poked fun, belittled or brought them under suspicion. Other times I outright called them out or declared my hope for their demise. Honestly, I didn't feel very godly during any of this. I was in the flesh.

While reading Acts 5, I was reminded of something a great man of God, Ron Mehl, once said to a group of pastoral leaders that included me. He was talking about his many years in ministry and all the waves of teaching, styles and flavors of church that had come and gone in the body of Christ. During those times folks would question why he and his church didn't "rides the waves."

Mehl humbly told us that many of the movements that arose over his years in ministry were no longer viable. They had died. The bubble burst. The wave crashed.

In the end, what is still standing?

I think that Gamaliel nailed it. If God is in it then you won't be able to stop it. If He's not, then it won't last.

That's not to say that the "waves" that did not last were not of God, but rather, it is to say that I have become increasingly careful to not be too quick to pronounce judgment.

The last thing I want to be said of my life is that I opposed God.

*–John Fehlen, pastor of West Salem Foursquare Church in Oregon.*

### Discussion Points:

1. Do you get the impression that Gamaliel was defending Peter and the other followers of Jesus who were on trial? Why or why not?

2. How can the words of Gamaliel influence our response to trendy and popular but questionable ministries?

3. From your experience watching ministries rise and fall, identify some of the important qualities of ministries that last.

### Prayer Points:

➤ Give me patience when I might otherwise be quick to judge the validity of another ministry.

➤ Lord, make clear to us the ministries You have established.

➤ Help me remain focused on the call You gave me so that I don't follow after tangents and distractions.

# ACTS 6

*"ARE WE DOING EVERYTHING WE CAN TO NOT
HOLD PEOPLE BACK, BUT TO RELEASE THEM
TOWARD ALL GOD HAS IN MIND?"*
**—TIM CLARK**

# ACTS 6: RESPONDING FULL OF THE SPIRIT AND WISDOM

BY JEFF ROPER

Bigotry, prejudice and discrimination made an unwelcomed appearance in the first-century church. It happened right in the middle of miracles, signs and wonders, and multitudes coming to Christ: "…here arose a complaint against the Hebrews by the Hellenists, because their widows were neglected in the daily distribution" (Acts 6:1, NKJV).

Had I been in charge that day, I might have preached on the evils of bigotry, then recruited volunteers to collect day-old bread from local bakeries and appointed a few administratively gifted people to ensure the food would be distributed fairly.

I am glad I was not there that day. I would have made a mess of things.

The issue wasn't food distribution. The issue was overcoming an obstacle to the gospel's advancement. Rather than addressing the people's prejudice, the apostles engaged in serving as the means of dominion. They practiced "overcoming evil with good."

The Hellenists and the Hebrews had to select from among themselves "seven men of good reputation, full of the Holy Spirit and wisdom" (v. 3). These men had to be Spirit-filled, wise and trusted, because their service would address deep-seated issues of prejudice, bigotry and discrimination.

In caring for those on the edge of survival, we often face the darkest parts of our humanity and the overwhelming lack of material resources. No wonder these men needed to be "of good reputation, full of the Holy Spirit and wisdom" (v. 3).

Kingdom expansion was immediate: "Then the word of God spread, and the number of the disciples multiplied greatly in Jerusalem, and a great many of the priests were obedient to the faith" (v. 7).

Reflecting on this experience, I ask myself:

- What crisis do I face that is really a Holy Spirit opportunity disguised in human brokenness?

- Am I making room for the miraculous in the daily demands of ministry?

- What lifestyle disciplines do I need to cultivate that will result in me being full of the Holy Spirit, wisdom, grace and power?

- Are there any long-term, latent issues in my heart that are hindering kingdom expansion?

Acts 6 powerfully illustrates that there is always more going on than what I see. Undercurrents, agendas and human frailty mingle with the goodness and blessing of God.

Like the disciples, we need men and women "to be full of the Spirit and wisdom" who can help us face our issues and move forward. Jesus, help me to be one of them.

*–Jeff and Debbie Roper, Foursquare Missions Europe area missionaries.*

### Discussion Points:

1. Describe a crisis you have faced that was really a Holy Spirit opportunity disguised in human brokenness.

2. What lifestyle disciplines do you need to cultivate that will result in being full of the Holy Spirit, wisdom, grace and power?

3. Honestly evaluate the condition of your heart, and share any issues that you identify that might hinder kingdom expansion.

---

**Prayer Points**

- Show me, Lord, how to make room for the miraculous in
my daily routine.

- Instill in me the personal disciplines I need to be full of Your wisdom, grace and power.

- Purge me of any residue of prejudice or arrogance, and fill me with Your Spirit.

# ACTS 6: PRAYING FOR DEEP CHANGE

BY REMI LAWANSON

It was in 1999 in Kampala, Uganda, while running a leadership and resource development workshop for denominational leaders, mission executives of Christian nonprofit organizations, seminary provosts and leaders of government agencies from different nations in East Africa that the Holy Spirit gave me a good understanding of Acts 6:1-7.

Prior to 1999, the church in Uganda (including The Foursquare Church) had been applying these concepts from Acts 6 leading to its transformation from slow death to deep change.

Uganda became the first nation in the world to experience a positive reversal of fortune with a drop in percentage of the population with HIV and thereby ceased to be the nation with the highest HIV infection per population (UNAIDS report on the global AIDS epidemic).

Other nations have other stories in other areas of life where the church is experiencing transformation from incremental to deep change. For example, in Cambodia, Canada, Cote d'Ivoire, Indonesia, Kenya, Brazil, Nigeria, Philippines, Singapore, South Africa, South Korea, United Kingdom, USA and Vietnam I have seen some churches and mission agencies move from incremental change and its slow death consequences to more ministry impact and growth.

Whenever I read Acts 6 and Robert Quinn's classic book, *Deep Change*, I desire that every one of us in our Foursquare family will experience biblical freedom from the trap of incremental change, especially its limitation and slow death. With this freedom, I pray that we are transformed through redemptive deep change so the Word of God will spread, the number of Jesus' disciples will increase rapidly, and leaders will become obedient to the faith (Acts 6:7).

From Acts 6, skills needed to move from incremental change to deep change include:

- Ministry Skills—spending time in prayer and teaching the Word—both, and not either/or. Many of us spend good time in teaching, but little or inadequate time in prayer. It is time for deep change.

- Relationship Skills—being connected with people. Relationship enhances ministry.

- Management Skills—for good biblical stewardship. Engage in holistic ministry. Remember Jesus Christ is described as full of grace and truth, not truth alone (John 1:14).

- Leadership Skills—casting vision, creating systems, crafting policies and giving direction. Develop leaders and not only followers. Developing followers leads to growth by addition, while developing leaders leads to growth by multiplication.

My fervent prayer for us is that we will continue to move from incremental to deep change, in Jesus' name.

*–Remi Lawanson, Greater Los Angeles District missions representative.*

**Discussion Points:**

1. In what ways do you think the Holy Spirit wants to improve your relationship skills with others?

2. What does good biblical stewardship look like in your life and ministry, especially in the realm of management skills?

3. Identify and explain specific steps you need to take to better develop leaders rather than only followers.

**Prayer Points:**

▸ Help me not to settle for merely a changed life, but also to strive for transformation.

▸ Father, equip me with the skills necessary to live a life of deep change.

▸ Lord, increase the number of Your disciples as Your children discover deep change.

# ACTS 6: ATTRIBUTES THAT PARTNER WITH GOD

BY TIM CLARK

In Acts 6 there is a serious leadership bottleneck. The church had been growing explosively (a good thing), but everyone was complaining about bad systems that led to broken community (a bad thing). Something had to be done before the whole thing blew up.

So the apostles called the rapidly expanding congregation to choose some people to serve, to organize, to manage and to care. And the infant church grew even more quickly. And everyone was happy.

It could have stopped there. Often as leaders we perceive we are doing our job well when we assign people to tasks that fit them. Moreover, when we see fruit from those decisions, we feel satisfied that our leadership direction really must be working.

But leadership isn't just about getting people plugged into the right slots. Stephen might have been called out for, and even gifted to "wait on tables" (Acts 6:2, NIV), but he was soon doing signs and wonders, preaching by the power of the Holy Spirit.

He was out changing the world.

Nowhere does the Bible indicate that this might have distressed the apostles. After Stephen was martyred, we don't find Peter and John saying, "If Stephen would have kept his mouth shut and stuck to waiting tables, this persecution wouldn't have broken out."

In fact, when reading further about some of these servants, I get the feeling that the growth of their ministry was celebrated.

Wherever we have influence, we have to develop a culture that releases people beyond the task to which they are assigned and that celebrates with them when they step out. We must provide an ethos of trust to workers in the church. Just because a person's job title says "nursery worker," "barista," "parking lot attendant" or "administrative pastor" doesn't mean the Holy Spirit doesn't want to move through him or her in powerful ways.

As believers we all do specific tasks and jobs as we serve one another, but we also worship a God who wants to work through us in amazing, world-changing, unimaginable ways.

Are we doing everything we can to not hold people back, but to release them toward all God has in mind? Are we partnering with God in His awesome intentions for the people we lead, or are we limiting them to be bound by our own unimaginative ideas of what they might be able to accomplish?

*–Tim Clark, district supervisor of the Greater Los Angeles District.*

### Discussion Points:

1. What does it take for a person to fully understand his or her personal mission from God?
2. As leaders how can we help in that process?
3. What directives or cautions do you see in Acts 6 about releasing people to specific ministry assignments in the body of Christ?

### Prayer Points:

- ▶ Keep my focus on what You want me to do with my time and for Your kingdom.

- ▶ Sharpen my vision that I might see the potential of others who serve with me.

- ▶ Make the pathway clear so that those I lead can easily follow You to their fullest potential.

# ACTS 7

*"GOD IS CALLING YOU TO A LIFE OF
HUMBLE SUBMISSION TO HIS WORD OVER YOU,
EVEN IF YOU DON'T FULLY UNDERSTAND IT.
YOU ARE A PERSON OF PROMISE AND A PERSON
OF BLESSING, AND GOD HAS AN AMAZING
FUTURE FOR YOU. IT MAY MEAN YOU HAVE
TO WALK AWAY FROM THE THINGS WITH
WHICH YOU ARE COMFORTABLE."*

*—SCOTT REECE*

# ACTS 7: HEADED TO CANAAN

BY SCOTT REECE

Abraham's father, Terah, had a vision of getting to Canaan, but he never made it. He ended up 400 miles away from his destination— that's about six hours away in today's travel. When Terah died, Abraham discovered a life of faith that was still talked about in New Testament days. In fact, it's how Stephen began his history of the Jewish people just before he was stoned as the first martyr of the church in Acts 7.

What Stephen meant as a testimony of God's faithfulness toward His people throughout the Old Testament has become a personal and prophetic word for us today. Let me share that word with you.

Stephen gives an account of several Old Testament patriarchs in order to make a case against those who were bringing charges against him. He begins with Abraham and his journey out of the land of Haran and into Canaan (see Gen. 12). Abraham was literally asked by the Lord to leave everything he had known, the people he had grown up with, and the life he was comfortable living. He was under a mandate to follow the Lord into a new land, full of unknowns, with nothing but the promise of God on his life.

It's interesting to me that in Gen. 11:31 we find Abraham's father setting out in similar fashion, heading toward Canaan. He brought his family as far as Haran and stopped there. Terah died in Haran, and Abraham entered into a brand-new season of opportunity, revelation and challenge.

Haran literally means, "to be scorched, charred, burnt, angry and dry." How many times have we ended up in places just like that? The trick of the enemy is to get us stuck in a place that is charred and scorched, and for us to end up dry and angry. Abraham faced that possibility, except for the Word of the Lord over him and his willingness to obey God and follow Him into the unknown.

With the promise of blessing on his life, Abraham set out to finish the job his father started. He was headed to Canaan!

The root word for Canaan is "Kana," which means to submit and to be humble. Wow! God had already released a blessing of promise on Abraham. In order for him to experience the fullness of that promise, he had to walk humbly before God. Abraham needed to submit to the Lord even when he did not understand all that was being asked of him.

Abraham discovered a life of faith that led him into unexpected blessings and opportunities to bless future generations. But Abraham's life isn't just ancient history. Even in today's circles, we talk about Abraham and how God sees us much like this great patriarch. We have that same promise of blessing on us today, according to Galatians 3:14. But, also like Abraham, sometimes we find ourselves in a place like Haran.

Maybe you have begun this new season, and it doesn't feel like a new season at all—it just feels like you're beating the same old drum, with just another chronological date attached to it. I'm here to tell you that God is calling you out of Haran! He may not be calling you to a different locale, but He is calling you out of a dry and angry season.

God is calling you to a life of humble submission to His word over you, even if you don't fully understand it. You are a person of promise and a person of blessing, and God has an amazing future for you. It may mean you have to walk away from the things with which you are comfortable.

Many times, my own comfort zone is what causes me the greatest amount of hindrance in my life. I must be open to new and fresh ways of doing things. I must be willing to allow God to bring new people into my life.

God's desire for you in this new season is that you would come into a new revelation for your life, a new insight into His calling and purposes for you and the ministry to which He has called you.

There are multitudes of families waiting for you to walk into the realization of the blessing that is on you. It's closer than you think, and you are the anointed of God for this season. His favor surrounds you on every side, even as a shield. God is for you, not against you.

You are headed to Canaan!

*–Scott Reece, supervisor of the Southeast District.*

### Discussion Points:

1. Evaluate and share how open you are to new and fresh ways of doing things and how willing you are to allow God to bring new people into your life.

2. Describe your response to this prophetic word: "There are multitudes of families waiting for you to walk in the realization of God's blessing that is on you."

3. What things in your life do you think God is calling you to set aside in order to experience the fullness of His purpose?

### Prayer Points

➤ Help me believe you, Lord, for a brand-new season of opportunity, revelation and challenge.

➤ Strengthen me to finish well all that You have started in me.

➤ Speak prophetically in and through me as I journey with You in this new season.

# ACTS 7: LIVING A WORLD-CHANGING LIFE

BY ROBB HATTEM

"I seek not a long life, but a full one, like You, Lord Jesus." –Jim Elliot (one of a team of missionaries murdered while serving in Ecuador in 1956)

Stephen undeniably lived fully and completely surrendered to Christ. As he stood before the Sanhedrin (see Acts 7), falsely accused and betrayed, God anointed him to proclaim that the gospel was for everyone, ultimately opening the way for the gospel to other peoples and cultures as described in Acts 1:8: " 'in Jerusalem, and in all Judea and Samaria, and to the end of the earth'" (NKJV).

Stephen didn't stand before the religious council, refuting the false testimony brought against him. Instead, he stood in the power of the Holy Spirit, proclaiming and prophesying, calling each of them into account.

As ministers we, like Stephen, are confronted with opposition at times, in the form of distrust, criticism, false accusation and even rejection. Sometimes we forget that we are engaged in a spiritual battle of the highest order, and one that can become very taxing. When the enemy is wearing us down with warfare, it can cut to the core of our being, tempting us to shrink back and not give ourselves completely.

I'm reminded of a time, several years ago, when I was in a dark place. I was very discouraged, hopeless and angry, believing nothing I did seemed to make any difference—I felt like giving up. In the middle of my "pity party," my close friend and assistant pastor strongly rebuked me, which shocked me out of my stupor.

"Pastor," he told me, "what you're saying isn't true!" He then vividly painted a picture of the transformation that was taking place in so many people in our congregation. As he shared, I became broken and undone by how desensitized my heart had become. I will always be thankful to God for that intervention—I almost missed the miracles of God that were right in front of me!

With his final breath, Stephen breathed the love of the Father: "Forgive them," he said (see v. 60).

Stephen saw the Lord Jesus stand as if to say, "I'm standing with you, and I'm standing to receive you" (see vv. 55-56) Nearby stood Paul— then Saul—who witnessed someone's life possessed by the life of the Spirit. Without a doubt this must have impacted Paul's life.

Because of Stephen's steadfast faithfulness, lives were changed, and a world was changed! The ministry that you and I have been entrusted with is making a world of difference, too—don't ever forget this!

"Fear not, for I am with you; be not dismayed, for I am your God. I will strengthen you, yes, I will help you, I will uphold you with My righteous right hand," (Is. 41:10, NKJV).

*–Robb Hattem, district supervisor of Foursquare's Northeast District.*

### Discussion Points:

1.  What has God shown you about your life and ministry that welcomes His life-changing presence?

2.  Describe any steps you have recently taken toward more of God and His fullness.

3.  In what ways have you struggled with fear or unbelief, and how have you conquered them in Christ?

### Prayer Points:

➤ Remind me of the impact of Your life in me, impacting the lives of others.

➤ When I become discouraged because of circumstances, show me what really matters.

➤ Strengthen my inner discipline that I won't be distracted by hindrances and temptations.

# ACTS 7: THREE THINGS I NEVER WANT TO BE

BY LOUIE D. LOCKE

Three things I never want to be: stiff-necked, hardened in my heart and resistant to the Holy Spirit.

"You stiff-necked and uncircumcised in heart and ears! You always resist the Holy Spirit; as your fathers did, so do you. Which of the prophets did your fathers not persecute? And they killed those who foretold the coming of the Just One, of whom you now have become the betrayers and murderers, who have received the law by the direction of angels and have not kept it," (Acts 7:51-53, NKJV).

Reading over this section of Scripture, I keep getting stuck on verse 51. Stiff-necked. Uncircumcised hearts. Resisters of the Holy Spirit.

These are strong and prophetic words from Stephen, who reached into Israel's history to challenge and rebuke the Jewish Religious Council for their opposition to God's purposes. The hardest thing for the Jewish leaders to hear had to be that their actions were just the latest round of thousands of years of stubborn, hard-hearted resistance to God. And the bizarre thing was, they professed to be diligently and faithfully serving the very One who was correcting them through Stephen.

Several things stand out to me:

- As Stephen is being dragged to the place of execution, the Jewish leaders have covered up their ears as though by doing so, they can keep from hearing anything else Stephen says. Their response to his prophetic challenge graphically portrays the state of their hearts and minds to which Stephen was testifying.

- To be stiff-necked is to be unteachable, stubborn, hardened and resistant to correction. Each time this phrase is used in Scripture, it refers to a willful, determined disobedience to God's specific commands, directions and ways.

- Stubborn resistance to God's purposes and plans originates in our own hearts, minds and wills, but it is hellishly motivated as well. This is evidenced by the vicious and murderous responses to the prophets and to Christ that Stephen recounts from Israel's history.

I want to be teachable, set apart to God in words and deeds so that I can easily be directed by and responsive to the leading of the Holy Spirit. This requires that I keep a close watch on my heart—that I cultivate humility and a lifestyle of repentance. And that I never forget that no matter how long I've followed the Lord, I never get to the spot where I don't desperately need His guidance, direction and grace.

*–Louie D. Locke, senior pastor of Fountainhead Foursquare Church in Carson City, Nev.*

### Discussion Points:

1. Have you ever felt like Stephen just before he was stoned to death? Or, have you ever felt like his religious opponents? What observations can you make about those feelings?

2. What does it take for a person to be fully teachable and responsive to the Holy Spirit?

3. Identify three things that you never want to be.

### Prayer Points:

- I promise to keep a close guard on my heart, Lord, so that I hear and follow Your leading.

- Make every day of my walk with You a fresh start, with new mercies each morning.

- My focus is to remain teachable and responsive to Your Spirit; help me remain faithful.

# ACTS 8

*"STILL, IN THE MIDDLE OF THEIR FLIGHT, [THE CHURCH] HAD THE SURETY OF GOD'S PROMISED HOLY SPIRIT, INDWELLING THEM, FILLING THEM WITH STRENGTH TO KEEP GOING AND BOLDNESS TO KEEP SHARING THE GOSPEL."*
*—LOUIE D. LOCKE*

# ACTS 8: REACHING PEOPLE OTHERS HATE

BY JIM SCOTT

Stephen's martyrdom changed everything for the early church.

Until this time, persecution of the church focused mainly on the leaders. Then Saul's participation in Stephen's execution and passionate commitment to destroy the church signaled a new attack. Now believers and leaders alike could be arrested, imprisoned and even killed (see Acts 7:58; 8:1-3).

So the persecuted and Spirit-baptized church was scattered from Jerusalem, and it was time for Philip to get out of town. He fled to the "ends of the earth," becoming an evangelist and a cross-cultural missionary (see Acts 8:4-5; 21:8) when God sent him to a Samaritan city.

However, the Samaritans and the Jews hated one another. Philip was probably raised in this hatred and prejudice. He chose to minister to the Samaritans irrespective of these huge and offensive differences. Philip intentionally crossed cultural and religious boundaries to evangelize Samaritan people.

To the Jews, Samaritans were a mixed Israelite-Assyrian people who were considered impure and non-Jewish. They worshiped in their own temple at Mount Gerazim, and this was such an offense to the Jews that they destroyed it in 127 B.C. Jews and Samaritans disagreed on the text of the Scriptures, on religious history and on the interpretation of the Scriptures.

The apostle John was significantly understating the Jewish-Samaritan hatred when he commented that Jews do not associate with Samaritans (see John 4:9). But Luke reveals the depth of this loathing as he tells us that both James and John wanted to call down "fire from heaven" on a Samaritan village that refused to welcome Jesus (see Luke 9:51-56).

Philip proclaimed the Good News of Jesus Christ to the Samaritans, and apparently they listened. "When the crowds heard Philip and saw the signs he performed, they all paid close attention to what he said" (Acts 8:6, NIV). He proclaimed that Christ is the Messiah, and this would have made sense to them, for they were looking for Him to come (see John 4:25).

Luke tells us that there was great joy in the city, because Philip did more than preach; he declared that the Messiah had come with healing and deliverance for all who believe. And, the Messiah healed and delivered people even as Philip spoke!

Church leaders in Jerusalem were astonished when they heard that the Samaritans accepted the Word of God. So much so, they sent Peter and John to join Philip. The Lord used John, one of the men who wanted to "call fire down" on a Samaritan village, to minister the baptism in the Holy Spirit to these Samaritans. Imagine how far John had come since that hateful request in Luke 9.

God is so redemptively confrontational.

Jesus promised that His people would receive power when the Holy Spirit came upon them. He said they would be His witnesses from Jerusalem to the ends of the earth. With this worldwide call in view, it's important to realize that this Samaritan city was within the borders of Israel.

The call was global; yet Philip was an evangelist and cross-cultural missionary at home.

Likewise, we have "Samaritans" within our borders today. We need to become more cross-culturally aware if they are to hear the Good News and be touched by the love of God. These people are different by their look, their religion or their birthplace. They are sometimes hated because of their politics or the policies of their nation of origin. Yet they are here—God has brought them here—and Jesus is asking us to be His witnesses among them.

It is a witness of word, and because we have received power, it is a witness of God's mighty acts through us. As in the Samaritan city where God used Philip, the days are coming when we will experience great joy in our cities.

God's promise is to heal and deliver when we choose to go!

*–Jim Scott, vice president of Foursquare Global Operations and director of Foursquare Missions International.*

## Discussion Points:

1. In what ways has the love of God compelled you to attempt to reach people who are looked down upon or regarded as a political or social "enemy"?

2. What specific steps will you take to become more cross-culturally aware?

3. How will you explain to your critics this commitment to reach "different" people with the love of Christ?

### Prayer Points

- Make me aware, Lord, of people that I have looked down on and maybe even hated.

- Cleanse my heart of attitudes that are in conflict with Your character.

- Show me ways to demonstrate Your tangible love for people who are different from me.

# ACTS 8: FAITH THAT WITHSTANDS ADVERSITY

BY LOUIE D. LOCKE

The martyrdom of Stephen instigated a firestorm of persecution against Christians, and the thousands of members of the Jerusalem church were faced with the choice: be imprisoned (or worse) or run. They ran.

"…At that time a great persecution arose against the church which was at Jerusalem; and they were all scattered throughout the regions of Judea and Samaria, except the apostles. … Therefore those who were scattered went everywhere preaching the word" (Acts 8:1b, 4, NKJV).

As they fled for their lives, I wonder if Jesus' last words to His disciples rang in their ears: "But you shall receive power when the Holy Spirit has come upon you; and you shall be witnesses to Me in Jerusalem, and in all Judea and Samaria, and to the end of the earth" (Acts 1:8).

Because, it was happening. They were now going throughout Judea. Samaria. To the ends of the earth. And everywhere they went, they were preaching the Word and sharing the gospel.

I bet they didn't think it would be like that. Still, in the middle of their flight, they had the surety of God's promised Holy Spirit, indwelling them, filling them with strength to keep going and boldness to keep sharing the gospel. Grace. Repentance. Forgiveness of sins. New life in Christ.

Even while on the run.

Even when we're walking through the valley of the shadow of death.

Even when the whole world seems to be turned upside-down.

Our faith in Christ is precisely for such times of adversity; our need for a Savior is never so obvious as when we're faced with suffering and difficulty. It is at these moments we discover the depth and breadth of what it means to have a rock of salvation in Christ—a hope that goes beyond this life and a peace that goes beyond understanding, that transcends circumstances.

*-Louie D. Locke, senior pastor of Fountainhead Foursquare Church in Carson City, Nev.*

### Discussion Points:

1. What is our reaction to persecution today? Withdrawing? Running? Speaking out? Fighting back?

2. How does your faith need to grow so that you can effectively withstand adversity?

3. How important is our hope in an eternal Savior when we face persecution?

### Prayer Points:

➤ Make me aware, Lord, of people whom I have looked down on and maybe even hated.

➤ Cleanse my heart of attitudes that are in conflict with Your character.

➤ Show me ways to demonstrate Your tangible love for people who are different from me.

# ACTS 8: BRINGING JOY TO YOUR CITY

BY JOHN FEHLEN

"For unclean spirits, crying with a loud voice, came out of many who were possessed; and many who were paralyzed and lame were healed. And there was great joy in that city" (Acts 8:7-8, NKJV).

There was much joy in that city. Did you catch that? Joy in the city.

This concept captivates my heart. What would it be like to have a city full of joy because of the life of Jesus and the proclamation of the gospel? When Phillip brought the message of Christ to the people of Samaria, it had a considerable effect upon them.

Unclean spirits were cast out. Paralyzed and lame people were healed. And, there was a notable sense of joy in the city.

That puts a smile on my face. I am captivated by the idea that a city could resonate with the life of Jesus to the degree that there is a tangible tone of joy. Does the message that we proclaim today have a similar effect?

If not, then perhaps we've forgotten that the Good News is supposed to be—well—good news.

What would "joy in the city" look like in the place you live?

*–John Fehlen, pastor of West Salem Foursquare Church in Oregon.*

### Discussion Points:

1. When was the last time you experienced a move of God in your community that resulted in divine joy?

2. What is it about the life of Jesus in people that can bring such joy to a city?

3. Are you open to hearing from the Holy Spirit how you might adjust your preaching to bring miracles and abundant joy to people?

### Prayer Points:

➤ Lord, transform my life and fill me with Your joy.

➤ Hover over my community, Holy Spirit, and meet the needs of people around me.

➤ Give me creative ways to share the joy and good news of Your gospel.

# ACTS 9

*"WHEN WE COVET THE PRESENCE OF THE LORD MORE THAN WE COVET COMFORT OR PRACTICALITY, THE STAGE IS SET FOR A MIGHTY MOVE OF THE HOLY SPIRIT."*

*—GLENN BURRIS JR.*

# ACTS 8-9: COVET GOD'S PRESENCE

BY GLENN BURRIS JR.

Acts 8 and 9 both begin by describing the intense persecution surrounding the church. Yet despite the constant threats upon their lives and families, the church, though scattered, thrived.

It seems likely that the persecution separated the serious followers from the casual ones. Despite the surrounding cultural climate, the church made great advances.

It appears as though tough times actually end up forcing the church to decide what its priorities are. While challenging situations seem to make or break us, they also tend to reveal our true motives and expose the depth of our commitments.

I was recently ministering for the first time in India and Sri Lanka with our national leaders, pastors and lay ministers. It was an eye-opening visit. The two countries, separated by the Indian Ocean, had once been provinces of Great Britain. Each of them won their independence in the 20th century.

Heavily influenced by Hinduism, Islam and Buddhism, these countries have become intense spiritual battlefields. The constant threat of imprisonment, harassment and even death are real. Our Foursquare campground in Sri Lanka was recently burned to the ground. In that country, you can't even put up a church sign.

In spite of these real challenges, the church is thriving. Miracle stories abound everywhere, and the resolve of church leaders is inspiring.

Our movement in India has tripled in the last 15 years, and in Sri Lanka, we are seeing the Lord change the spiritual landscape of the nation, one family at a time. Both have huge challenges, but the church there is focused, full of faith and committed to take the gospel to the ends of the earth. Sri Lankans are locating their people groups around the globe and planting churches where they are, including in emirate states such as Bahrain and Qatar.

During the evening services in Sri Lanka, blind eyes and deaf ears were opened. The testimonials went long into the night, with no one interested in leaving.

Habakkuk prayed this prayer: "O Lord, I have heard Your speech and was afraid; O Lord, revive Your work in the midst of the years! In the midst of the years make it known; in wrath remember mercy" (Habbakuk 3:2, NKJV).

Book-of-Acts-like stuff didn't just happen in places such as Samaria in the first century; it's happening now. It is taking place where people have the same hunger that the prophet Habakkuk did. When we covet the presence of the Lord more than we covet comfort or practicality, the stage is set for a mighty move of the Holy Spirit.

The current economic and political landscape has put us in a national crisis. The church could rise to be a voice of hope and reason. The church could provide a place of refuge and strength. Let's not be shaped by our current culture. Instead, let's influence it.

The church of Jesus Christ, this community of believers, has been called and anointed as God's strategy for redemption on the earth. The cry of our hearts should be to see an awakening of the fame and deeds of God—in our day, in our time, in our generation.

We desperately need a divine visitation of the Lord, but are we willing to pay the price for it?

*–Glenn Burris Jr., president of The Foursquare Church.*

**Discussion Points:**

1. What will it take for the church to become all God has promised it should be in the world?

2. Identify specific spiritual steps every believer must take in order for the church to fulfill its mission in the world.

3. Respond to this statement: "When we covet the presence of the Lord more than we covet comfort or practicality, the stage is set for a mighty move of the Holy Spirit."

**Prayer Points:**

➤ I want You, Lord, as much as Habakkuk did; please move!

➤ Use me to influence the culture around me and to not be influenced by it.

➤ I am willing to do whatever You want me to, Lord. I'm ready for your manifestation.

# ACTS 9: STAYING FLEXIBLE—GOD MAY HAVE ANOTHER PLAN

BY GUILLERMO PUPPO

Saul had a well-laid plan to persecute Christians and bring them bound to Jerusalem—but God had a different plan.

The narrative in Acts 9 describes the encounter between Saul and Jesus Christ (see Acts 9:3), in which the brightness of the light of Christ surrounded Saul and made him fall to the ground. It wasn't only Saul's physical body that hit the ground—so did his plans and his belief system. His whole life fell to the ground, being struck by the glorious light of the truth incarnate: Jesus Christ.

Saul finally arrived in Damascus, but in a very different way than he had planned. He was going to break others, but instead he was broken. He was going to watch others, but instead he was blinded. He was going to bring death, but instead he received Life, Jesus Himself. Saul searched to find something, but instead was found by God.

The people Saul intended to attack helped heal him and protect him (see Acts 9:17, 25), and he ended up boldly and passionately proclaiming the name he had tried to eliminate and walking the way he had tried to destroy.

I don't know about you, but for me, that is quite a change of plans!

We all have our Damascus, our plans and our agendas. Our plans are perhaps not as violent as Saul's, but they are still based on what we believe and look forward to achieving. Often we think these plans are the best we can do to "help" God do His work on Earth.

When reading Acts 9, I can only pray and ask God that in my road to Damascus I also may be intercepted by His Son, captivated by His glory, challenged by His truth and clothed with His Spirit. I pray that my schedule and my plans will be forever altered by His wisdom, prompting me to proclaim the name of Jesus with passion and courage wherever I am.

*–Guillermo Puppo, an administrative assistant to Ted Vail, one of Foursquare Missions International's associate directors.*

### Discussion Points:

1.  As with the Apostle Paul when he first encountered Jesus Christ on the Damascus Road, how have your plans and expectations changed since you first met Jesus?
2.  What is your response when God sends you in a different direction than you thought you would go?
3.  How do you remain focused and spiritually stable when plans around you change?

### Prayer Points:

➤ If my plans are different from Yours, Lord, show me how to align my life with Your plans.

➤ Keep me motivated only by Your Spirit and Your Word and not by my will.

➤ Do great things through me as I am fully surrendered to Your guidance.

# ACTS 9: WALKING IN HEALTHY FEAR AND ENCOURAGEMENT

BY TIM CLARK

"Then the churches throughout all Judea, Galilee, and Samaria had peace and were edified. And walking in the fear of the Lord and in the comfort of the Holy Spirit, they were multiplied" (Acts 9:31, NKJV).

Though I don't think the measure of a church's impact can be primarily evaluated by its attendance, I am always interested in the context surrounding the early church's increase in numbers, because that increase was unwaveringly due to new believers coming to Christ.

If we take Acts seriously, we will learn to both count and celebrate large amounts of people coming to faith in Jesus. In chapter 9 we find one of nearly twenty references in Acts to the numerical growth of the church. And I think we can learn something about the conditions in which that growth occurred.

In a single verse, the Bible declares that the church was "living in the fear of the Lord" and that it was "encouraged [or comforted] by the Holy Spirit." Fear and encouragement—these two things don't seem to mix. Especially when you tie them directly to church growth!

So much of our strategy regarding church expansion and health seems to fall into one of these two camps:

1. **Encouragement and Comfort.** This is all about the imminence of God. These folks want people to know an infinitely kind and all-loving Father. Jesus can be our true best friend and even our buddy. He is accessible to us through the Holy Spirit and is always available to help us with anything we might need.

2. **The fear of the Lord.** This is all about the transcendence of God. This group is concerned with people understanding how big and awesome God

is. We serve a totally just Father-judge, and Jesus is a warrior-king who won't put up with sloppy living. The Holy Spirit exists to bring conviction, as well as salvation, which is for His glory alone.

Depending on which approach we take, our church growth/health strategies will look very different.

So, which is it, transcendence or imminence? Is God magnificent, unsurpassed and beyond understanding, or does He reveal Himself to us as personal, intimate, affectionate and a revealer of the secrets of His nature?

In Acts, we find that the early church embraced God's transcendence as well as His imminence. If they only knew His comfort, they would neglect His power; if they only walked in the fear of the Lord, they would lose a vital grasp of how much He loved them.

Let's keep that balance, too. We can and should live as churches that walk in both the fear and the encouragement of the Lord, that see many come to Jesus because they find through us how loving and how powerful God truly is.

*–Tim Clark, district supervisor of the Greater Los Angeles District.*

**Discussion Points:**

1. What is your response to the idea from Acts 9 of walking in both fear and encouragement?

2. How do these two seemingly contradictory ideas result in healthy church growth?

3. In what ways does your church's growth strategy involve both a loving and a powerful God?

**Prayer Points:**

- My life must reflect healthy balance, and I trust You to help me walk in that health.

- Show me what my church should look like as we strive for godly balance.

- Grow Your people and Your church so we align with Your purpose and call.

# ACTS 10

*"WHAT WOULD HAVE HAPPENED IF PETER HAD NOT TAKEN TIME TO PRAY? HE WOULD HAVE MISSED OUT ON THIS HUGE AND GOD-INTENDED BREAKTHROUGH. WHAT HAPPENS IF WE DON'T TAKE TIME TO PRAY, HEAR THE LORD AND FOLLOW HIS INSTRUCTION?"*

*—KIMBERLY DIRMANN*

# ACTS 10: EMBRACING CHANGE BELOW THE SURFACE

BY GLENN BURRIS JR.

Robert E. Quinn wrote a book titled *Deep Change*, and I would highly recommend it if you want to be open to new possibilities.

In it, Quinn outlines fundamental behaviors that are consistent with an individual or an organization going through not just surface change, but deep change as well.

The old adage says it's insanity to think that you can continue to do the same things but expect different results.

Quinn specifies that deep change will adhere to the following characteristics:

1. Is major in scope
2. Is discontinuous with the past
3. Is generally irreversible
4. Distorts existing patterns of actions
5. Involves taking risks
6. Means surrendering control

Change for change's sake is rarely, if ever, helpful. However, there are traits that tend to identify whether or not a leader is headed in the right direction with his or her life and ministry.

If you find a leader who is open, responsive, teachable and willing to submit to the work of the Spirit, then you will find a leader heading in the right direction. But if you find a leader who is resistant, closed and often rigid, you will discover someone who is in dire need of a fresh move of the Holy Spirit. These traits in a leader's life determine if he or she is part of the solution or part of the problem.

In Acts 10, Peter was entrenched in a certain way of thinking (like most of us) until a vision from the Lord broke in on his thinking.

There is a fine line between spiritual convictions that are timeless and born of the Spirit, and our personal convictions that often have been developed out of our own experiences and perspectives. Peter yielded to the instruction of the angel who appeared to him, although the Lord decided that Peter needed to hear the instruction three times. Don't you love it!

Cornelius was a God-fearing, generous, devout and prayerful man, but like Peter he was also in need of some adjustments. He was a centurion in an Italian regiment and had earned a stellar reputation, even among the Jews. In a vision, an angel told Cornelius to send for Peter.

When Peter arrived, Cornelius said, "…Therefore, we are all present before God, to hear all the things commanded you by God" (Acts 10:33, NKJV). That openness led to an outpouring of the Spirit on all of those who had gathered and to an explosion of the gospel to the gentile world. They even got baptized in the Holy Spirit before they got baptized in water. You've got to applaud God's style! He delights in rearranging our protocols.

God isn't opposed to challenging our practices or our thinking, but He is interested in removing any obstacles that prevent us from being effective. He wants to go deep and bring about change that is transformational. He will instruct, confront, rebuke and even allow us to experience the consequences of our own choices in order to bring us to a place of humility and recognition that we need Him above all else.

Choose today to be moldable clay in the hands of the Master Potter, and get ready for Him to do something that even heaven will celebrate.

–Glenn Burris Jr., president of The Foursquare Church.

### Discussion Points:

1. How many of the traits of deep change do you identify in your life?

2. Are you part of the solution or part of the problem?

3. Name particular changes you need to make to fully embrace health, strength and growth in your life, your family and your ministry.

### Prayer Points

- ➤ Help me listen carefully that I will be able to hear all that You are saying.

- ➤ Instruct, confront and rebuke me so I am transformed into Your likeness.

- ➤ Mold me, Lord, into something that heaven can celebrate.

# ACTS 10: KNOWING AND FOLLOWING THE VOICE OF THE LORD

BY KIMBERLY DIRMANN

There is no doubt that Peter, the most prominent person in the Jerusalem church, had a lot on his mind and that the reports of the supernatural surrounding his ministry would cause many in Joppa to seek his counsel or prayer. In spite of all the other demands on his time, Peter took time—by himself—to pray (see Acts 10:9).

I'm sure that as Peter went up to the roof of that house to pray, he had no idea that God was going to speak a word to him that would forever alter both the course of his ministry and the future of the church at large.

Although Peter did not initially understand the vision nor the accompanying words from the Lord, he didn't dismiss the experience, saying, "That was weird!" He continued to ponder and wait for its meaning. That's when the Holy Spirit spoke to him with clear and practical direction.

Because Peter followed the instructions he received in prayer and did not lean on his own understanding (see Prov. 3:5-6), the barrier that confined the gospel of Jesus Christ and the power of the Holy Spirit—both to the Jews and from the rest of the world—was destroyed.

What would have happened if Peter had not taken time to pray? He would have missed out on this huge and God-intended breakthrough. What happens if we don't take time to pray, hear the Lord and follow His instruction?

It is useless to argue with the words of Jesus: " 'How much more will your Father who is in heaven give good things to those who ask Him!' " (Matt. 7:11, NKJV).

In John 4:35 Jesus said, "Behold, I say to you, lift up your eyes and look at the fields, for they are already white for harvest!"

The Head of the church knows the fields; He knows where the harvest is, and He knows how to gather them. There is no shortage of harvest and no shortage of people who are ready to become disciples of Christ. But we need both to know where to look and the divine direction to gather them.

We must never forget that God is not passive about building His church. He already has a plan, and His plan always works. So, what difference could it make today if you received just one word from God?

*–Kimberly Dirmann, district supervisor of Foursquare's Southwest District.*

### Discussion points:

1. Describe a circumstance in which you clearly heard and obeyed the word of the Lord?

2. What would have happened in that circumstance if you had not taken time to hear the voice of the Lord?

3. What specific skill has God shown you in order to minister to the people He has called you to reach?

### Prayer Points:

▸ Prompt me, Lord, to seek You until I fully understand the vision You give me.

▸ Forgive me for my insensitivity to Your plan, and use me in that plan today.

▸ Show me how to bring people to maturity in Christ right where I live.

# ACTS 10: WHEN GOD ASKS THE UNTHINKABLE

BY TIM CLARK

In Acts 10, God asks Peter to do the unthinkable. Peter is going to need to have fellowship with and share Jesus' message with … gentiles. And the way it's all revealed to Peter is through a divine invitation to dig into a big meal made entirely of unclean food. Peter had never done either of those things!

What Peter didn't know was that the Lord was about to unfold His eternal plan that had been in process for ages (see Ephesians 2), to bring the gentiles into family relationship with the Jews as they all got in on the Good News.

Better yet, God would use Peter as the spark that would get this whole fire burning.

Imagine if Peter had said: "No way! God doesn't work like that. And even if He does, that really isn't my calling; it doesn't fit with my gifting; it isn't what I'm wired to do."

Now, I do believe the Lord has a unique calling for each of us and that He has hard-wired certain gifts and God-given-abilities into our personalities. For some reason, ultra-Pharisee Paul would end up being the apostle to the gentiles just as Peter would be the apostle to the Jews (Gal. 2:8). And for reasons God only knew, that fit them each perfectly.

But God also planned to use Peter as the one through whom the gentiles would first receive the gospel. Though it wasn't his thing, as a postmodern gentile, I'm sure glad that Peter was obedient and flexible to accept an assignment that seemed out of his depth.

It was only a single assignment, but what an assignment!

When we are inflexible and unmoving about what we will and won't do for God, we can miss some awesome opportunities.

So, by all means, do find your shape, know and understand your personality type, grip your Birkman assessment, comprehend your gift mix—and then, when it's all said and done, submit yourself each day to whatever the Lord would do through you to touch your world, even when—maybe especially when—it doesn't all make sense.

*–Tim Clark, district supervisor of the Greater Los Angeles District.*

**Discussion Points:**

1. What unthinkable thing has God asked of you recently?

2. How did you respond, and what happened as a result?

3. In what ways do your strengths or gifts enhance God's call on your life? In what ways do they conflict with that call?

**Prayer Points:**

➤ When You call me to do something I've never done before, I will say, "Yes," and will go.

➤ Even though I think I know my gifting, use me in whatever way You want to, Lord.

➤ Rather than waiting for Your call to make sense to me, I promise to listen and respond when You prompt me to minister.

# ACTS 11

*"MY PRAYER TODAY IS THAT I RECEIVE A FRESH VISION FROM THE LORD THAT WILL PROPEL ME OUT OF MY COMFORT ZONE AND INTO HIS PERFECT WILL."*
—*STERLING BRACKETT*

# ACTS 11: GET UP AND GO, CHURCH

BY DAVE VEACH

"When I observed it intently and considered, I saw four-footed animals of the earth, wild beasts, creeping things, and birds of the air. And I heard a voice saying to me, 'Rise, Peter; kill and eat.' But I said, 'Not so, Lord! For nothing common or unclean has at any time entered my mouth.' But the voice answered me again from heaven, 'What God has cleansed you must not call common'" (Acts 11:6-9, NKJV).

How much of Peter's resistance to the Lord's leading was theological? How much was culturally influenced? His desire was to adhere to the Jewish laws, and they were clearly laid out for him. Contradicting those laws would fly in the face of his community. "Surely not, Lord," is a response I know all too well. Often, a fresh word from the Lord can seem contrary to what I've already accepted as His will for me. One would think that after walking with Jesus for this many years, I wouldn't hesitate to obey His promptings. Yet when the "get up, kill and eat" kind of instructions come to me, I am quick to remind the Lord, "Surely not! That would not be a good idea, because I'm occupied with what you already told me."

In 2009 my wife, Windy, and I relocated to the third-largest city in our state after having pastored for nearly 20 years on an island. Our home dramatically shifted from the once-tranquil cul-de-sac in the country with a mountain and water views to the pace and buzz of a city. My flatscreen TV hangs on a wall that is literally only four paces from a city bus stop.

Though we loved our assignment on the island, God beckoned us to the city. The demographic of people that we once sent missionaries to is now at the bus stop by my front door. The challenge for the Veaches is the challenge for all of us: "Get up, church, and go to the field that is now at your bus stop!"

"But Lord," we might say, "they are not my demographic; they look to be impure. This couldn't be your leading, could it?" We know we are all called to open our hearts with the love of Jesus to people, but we sometimes fight the urge to answer that call with, "Nothing impure near me!"

The fields are white across the globe as well as at our bus stops. Get up, church, rise, and love this lost and dying world to Jesus while this window of time is open; it might not be open much longer!

*–Dave Veach, district supervisor of the Northwest District.*

### Discussion Points:

1. How far are you willing to be stretched in order to "go" and reach people for God?

2. In what ways can we combat personal comfort as an excuse for Christians to ignore the world around them?

3. As you evaluate the need in your community and the people in your church, how likely is it that the church will be effective in reaching more people for Christ this year?

### Prayer Points:

➤ I need to really hear a "fresh word" from You, Lord.

➤ Show me the people You want me to touch in Your name, even if I never thought of them before.

➤ Purify my heart so I won't miss a moment to bless someone on Your behalf.

# ACTS 11: OPEN OUR EYES, LORD

BY STERLING BRACKETT

As I look at Acts 11, I am convinced that the Lord wants to impress upon us the importance of vision, because the first part of this chapter basically recounts the Acts 10 story of Peter's vision on the rooftop.

Peter's recounting the event was occasioned by the criticism of Judean believers who were aghast that gentiles had received the gospel. Peter, who had been just as amazed at Cornelius' rebirth, told the story in self-defense. The vision Peter received changed his life—and it changed the lives of all those in Cornelius' household.

I believe that a vision from the Lord will change our lives so that we can help change the lives and destinies of those who have yet to hear the good news of our Savior. When we receive a vision, we can no longer stay safely cocooned in the comfort of the familiar. A vision from God will lead us to places we have not yet explored, but also to a place our Lord has ordained us to be.

Jesus said, "I must be about my Father's business" (Luke 2:49, NKJV), and that business is redeeming lost people. Since He commended His earthly work to us, Jesus provides vision so that we can do the same works He did.

The Holy Spirit has pointedly made me aware that, at times, I am more concerned about my own preferences in life than about the lost men and women all around me.

My prayer today is that I receive a fresh vision from the Lord that will propel me out of my comfort zone and into His perfect will. A statement by M. David Sills in his book, *The Missionary Call*, jolted my heart as I read it: "I am haunted by the danger of living my life so that I will come to the end of it, look over my shoulder, and realize that I lived it in selfish comfort and convenience" (p. 176).

May God open our eyes and enable us to see the world through His.

*—Sterling Brackett, vice president, chief operating officer and corporate secretary for The Foursquare Church.*

### Discussion Points:

1. In what ways has a vision from God pried you out of your cocoon of comfort?

2. What do you do when the Holy Spirit points out that you care more about your own comfort than the salvation of others?

3. Describe a time when your spiritual vision was 20/20 and God used you to reach someone outside your comfort zone?

### Prayer Points:

- Transform my thinking so that I care more about others than I do about myself.

- Propel me, Lord, from my own selfishness toward Your will for my life.

- Live Your life through me today.

# ACTS 11: BEING GOD'S WITNESS TO ALL PEOPLE

BY LOUIE D. LOCKE

"Now those who were scattered after the persecution that arose over Stephen traveled as far as Phoenicia, Cyprus, and Antioch, preaching the word to no one but the Jews only. But some of them were men from Cyprus and Cyrene, who, when they had come to Antioch, spoke to the Hellenists, preaching the Lord Jesus. And the hand of the Lord was with them, and a great number believed and turned to the Lord" (Acts 11:19-21, NKJV).

The great persecution that followed the martyrdom of Stephen resulted in the scattering of believers—Jews and God-fearers—from Jerusalem to points all over the Roman world. Many even traveled as far as Antioch, a significant and strategic Roman colony about 300 miles to the north of Jerusalem.

And as they went, they preached the gospel, the Good News of repentance, the forgiveness of sins, and salvation available through the name of Jesus Christ for all who would believe.

What stood out to me as I read this chapter was that those fleeing persecution preached the gospel to most everyone they met. Most everyone that was like them, that is—they shared the Word only with fellow Jews. *Ouch.*

The problem was they were running through areas populated by predominantly Greek/non-Jewish peoples. It's normal, human even, to gravitate toward what we're familiar with—toward "people like us" with similar culture, interests and experiences. Though it may be easier and more comfortable to do so, Jesus' challenge to His followers in the Great Commission specifically says to do and live otherwise. When He told His followers that they would share the gospel in Jerusalem, Judea, Samaria and to the ends of the earth. He was implicitly stating that they would be witnesses to all people—not just the Jews, but everyone.

Fortunately, there were a few good men, Christ-following "outsiders" from Cyprus and Cyrene, who intentionally and faithfully declared the Good News message to everyone. And not only was this message declared, it was received with joy and fruitfulness, and "a great number" believed and "turned to the Lord."

My prayer is that the Holy Spirit—the One who fills us with power to live for Christ and to tell others of what we've seen, heard and experienced from Him—will remind us of the call to lift our eyes from what we know, from what and who we're comfortable with, to look to the fields that are white with harvest. The Lord is actively looking for men and women who will allow Him to work through them so He can gather people to Himself. Let's be a part of that.

Also, it's interesting to me to hear that Barnabas, the "son of encourage-ment" who was Paul's missionary companion for many years, was from Cyprus (an island off the coast of Ephesus). And Simon, the man who carried the cross for Christ on the way to Golgotha, was from Cyrene (in Northern Africa, most likely modern Libya.)

–Louie D. Locke, senior pastor of Fountainhead Foursquare Church in Carson City, Nev.

**Discussion Points:**

1. Have you ever been the object of personal prejudice? Have you ever been the person with prejudice?

2. How can we as Christians guard against showing prejudice when we share the gospel?

3. What does it mean in your circumstance to go to the ends of the earth with God's love?

**Prayer Points:**

▸ Release me to share Your limitless love with everyone I meet.

▸ Free me in Your Spirit to be Your witness everywhere I go.

▸ Challenge my comfort zones, Lord, and give me success reaching the world for Christ.

# ACTS 12

*"GOD IS ENDURINGLY AND ENDLESSLY
AND COMPLETELY GOOD... AND IT IS ONLY
IN FIRMLY TETHERING OUR SOULS TO THIS
BELIEF IN HIS GOODNESS THAT WE CAN
FACE THE WORLD WE LIVE IN..."*
*—KIM CECIL*

# ACTS 12: BECOMING AN UNSTOPPABLE FORCE FOR CHRIST

BY STERLING BRACKETT

A lot was going on in the early church, and life was never dull! Acts 12 begins with the martyrdom of the apostle James, the brother of John; Jesus had called these brothers "Sons of Thunder." But James would thunder no more. Herod Agrippa, grandson of Herod the Great, had had James ignominiously beheaded.

Furthermore, enjoying the favor of the people, Herod had yet another apostle, Peter, imprisoned and closely guarded. No doubt, he intended for Peter to meet a fate similar to that of James. What was this small group of believers to do? Twelve apostles had been commissioned to change the world with the good news of Jesus Christ—and now the number of apostles was down to 11.

Those events make the words recorded in verse five tremendously exciting: "…constant prayer was offered to God for him by the church" (NKJV). Peter was miraculously released from prison and restored to the group of believers in Jerusalem—and you know the rest of the story.

Herod's fate was not a happy one: an angel struck him down, and worms ate him (v. 23). This may have been a condition that ancient people called *morbus pedicularis* (taken from Barnes' notes on the Bible), an intestinal disease that probably killed Herod Agrippa's grandfather, Herod the Great—another tyrant who thought he could thwart God's plan.

"But the word of God grew and multiplied" (Acts 12:24). A praying church will withstand all the attacks of the enemy. A praying church will see the fulfillment of Tertullian's words, "The blood of the martyrs is the seed of the church." A praying church will experience miracles when it seems that disaster looms. A praying church will not be stopped by any hindrance that is placed in its way. A praying church is a triumphant church.

Will you join me in making a commitment to pray—whatever comes our way? As we follow the pattern of the early church and pray earnestly, we become part of an unstoppable force that God will use to bring salvation to the world.

*—Sterling Brackett, chief operating officer of The Foursquare Church.*

### Discussion Points:

1. In what ways has fervent prayer changed your life?
2. Describe miracles you have personally witnessed.
3. What will it take for you to see more people delivered, saved and healed?

**Prayer Points:**

▸ As I pray, help me see the work of the enemy thwarted.

▸ As I pray, help me see miracles when others only see disasters.

▸ As I pray, help me see victory in my life and in my church.

# ACTS 12: UNSHAKEN FAITH

BY CHRISTINA CHAO

I was deeply disturbed. My prayer closet had been filled with fervent, loud, sincere and forceful petitions without a single response from the Lord. God had not spoken to me for three weeks. As a senior pastor, I have ministered to many people struggling with the idea of faith, but now I was forced to answer the question: "What is faith to me?"

My family owns a small business, and sales had dropped 30 percent. Every morning I prayed fervently: "Lord, please keep our business up. I believe You will do this, because I am Your daughter, and You are my loving Father." Every night I prayed loudly: "Lord, please show me the problems in our business. I will correct them according to your will."

My fervent prayers reflected my simple faith: I believed, and I prayed. God would listen, and then I would receive. This is how it is supposed to work, isn't it?

Business continued to decline, and I began to analyze my simple faith. I thought my faith was too small, so I prayed more sincerely: "My Lord, You are in control of my personal life, church ministry and this business, too. Although I am not able to pay some of the bills now, I believe You are in control, and You will supply."

Then some of our equipment broke down and needed to be repaired. We had difficulty with permits, and I was preparing to leave for Asia on a ministry trip. My anxiety continued to rise. I began to pray forcefully: "We will conquer the enemy and win this battle!"

Difficult as it is, we have to admit how easy it is for us pastors to hide our own doubts and the weakness of our own faith. We know the words of God very well. We all can quote the right scriptures at the right time. We often convince ourselves that we believe in every word of God, don't we?

The day before my trip to Asia, I could not pray anymore, because I did not know what else I could say to the Lord. He had not spoken to me for three weeks, and a double dosage of high blood pressure medicine was my best friend.

While waiting for my flight at the airport, I cried out to the Father: "Lord, didn't I pray earnestly? Why can't I sleep like Peter did in Acts 12 when he was in prison? When can I be released from my chains like he was? Why can't I escape from my prison?"

I thought about how Peter's friends prayed for his release, but when he stood at their front door waiting to get inside, they did not believe he was free. Peter had been completely at peace, resting in the Lord while he was in prison, and his bondage was broken.

As my flight lifted off, I realized how often we pray in faith but then doubt the outcome. "Lord, I only want to be with You," I said. "I don't care if I am in prison or if I am chained. I only want to be with You."

I heard the voice of the Lord speaking to me: "Everything will turn around and be back to its goodness," He said. Later I discovered that, on that very day, our business began to increase again! Financial issues were solved, and problem machines were fixed. I was speechless but praised God: "Wow, Lord, You are the Great I Am!"

Faith is everything we have been taught from the pulpit and have discussed in Bible studies. But faith is also to experience Jesus Christ and to be with Him, and especially to find peace in Him. This is the unshaken faith.

*–Christina Chao is senior pastor of Home of Grace (Las Vegas Chinese Foursquare Church) in Las Vegas, Nev.*

**Discussion Points:**

1. Have you ever been so burdened by a situation in life that you thought you could not pray any more? What did you do and how did God answer?

2. What have you discovered about prayers that try to manipulate God?

3. How much time do you devote daily to simply being with the Lord?

**Prayer Points:**

▸ Guard my emotions, Lord, so I can fully believe You for everything I need.

▸ As I trust You in faith, let me also experience You fully.

▸ Help me set aside the concerns that can overwhelm me so I soak in all of You.

# ACTS 12: LIVING IN GOD WHEN WE CAN'T COMPREHEND

BY KIM CECIL

Acts 12 contains two stories juxtaposed curiously, at least to me: Peter's escape and James' martyrdom. This James we are reading of is the same one who was John's brother, one of the "Sons of Thunder," one of only three men to see the special transfiguration of Jesus on the mountain (see Mark 9:2). In our story we find that James becomes the second recorded Christian martyr in history, and his good buddy Peter is on the same path until an angel came to his rescue and walks him out of prison unnoticed. We have then two men, both with the same passion and zeal for Christ, both with a calling and anointing, both with extraordinary experiences with the physical Son of God to share with others, and one of them dies and the other lives.

These contrasting narratives remind me of what happened to two close friends of mine this summer. Overjoyed to have her first child in May 2009, one of the friends was pregnant again with a baby boy, due December 2010. In July the couple went for a routine checkup, and the nurse could not find the baby's heartbeat. Shaken and terrified we waited all afternoon for the results of the ultrasound. I waited—praying, anxious, pacing—until at 3 p.m. I got a text: "Our baby has gone to be with Jesus."

But that's not the end of the story. Later that summer I was speaking to my friends who had suffered this tragedy, and they proceeded to tell me that their own close friends in Ohio had the exact same thing happen just the week before; the pregnant wife had gone in, and the nurse could not find the baby's heartbeat. Like my friends they waited anxiously for the results of their ultrasound, crying out to God for a miracle.

However, similarly to our Acts 12 stories, their own ends differently: their baby ended up being fine. There was no indication of any reason why his heartbeat could not be found. Like Peter, this baby "escaped" his potential tragedy.

The obvious question these stories elicit is the same one that is swift and unavoidable and relentless in the face of all human tragedy: *"Why?"*

Like everyone on this side of heaven I do not have an answer to that question. What I do know is this: God is enduringly and endlessly and completely good. He is good when things go Hallmark-card splendidly and it seems we will live "happily ever after," and He is good when the dark night of the soul descends and the questions pile unrelentingly until they become insurmountable in our minds. And it is only in firmly tethering our souls to this belief in His goodness that we can face the world we live in, a world where it is possible for righteous men to die senselessly and children with unlimited potential to never get a chance at their first breath.

There is an end we cannot yet see or comprehend where "all things shall be made new" and "the dead shall be raised to new life" in our Savior, Jesus Christ. This is our hope, this is our joy, and this is our portion as saints of God. Until this comes fully to pass, we learn to "rejoice with those who rejoice, and weep with those who weep" (Rom. 12:15, NKJV). The rejoicing part seems simple enough, but to mourn well is perhaps more beautiful still.

*–Kim Cecil, Heartland District missions representative and co-pastor of The Journey (Madison-Metro Foursquare Church) with her husband, Steve.*

### Discussion Points:

1. In what ways can you identify with circumstances that are "beyond our comprehension?"

2. How would you explain God's will to a person who didn't understand why one person lives and another person dies?

3. What does the directive from Rom. 12:15 look like as you guide people through the grieving process?

**Prayer Points:**

‣ When "why" seems to be the only thing we can say, equip me to stand in unwavering faith.

‣ Enable in me the beauty of being able to mourn with those who mourn.

‣ Fill me with Your joy when others can celebrate, even when I can't.

# ACTS 13

*"SOMETIMES MY DESIRE TO BE LIKED CAN BECOME DISPROPORTIONATE TO THE GREATER CALLING ON MY LIFE: TO SHEPHERD PEOPLE TO JESUS WITH TRUTH SPOKEN OUT OF GENUINE LOVE BORN OF THE HOLY SPIRIT."*
**—CHRIS MANGINELLI**

# ACTS 13: DEALING WITH THE POPULARITY DILEMMA

BY CHRIS MANGINELLI

I like to be liked. It's definitely my preference. I'm guessing it's yours, too. God has equipped me with decent people skills and a good ear for listening. This often equates to favor with people. Sometimes, however, my desire to be liked can become disproportionate to the greater calling on my life: to shepherd people to Jesus with truth spoken out of genuine love born of the Holy Spirit.

In Acts 13, we jump into a marvelous story of the first missionary activity and the commissioning of Paul and Barnabas. As these heroes of our faith embrace their calling and zealously engage in the activity of their mission, I see some similarities between them and, um, … *us*.

Barnabas was a very likeable fellow. Throughout Acts, he seems to garner the favor of all. His very name means "son of encouragement." God gifted him to be generous of heart and resource, and no one benefited more from Barnabas' likeability than Paul. Paul's acceptance into the early church took place because Barnabas went to bat for him.

I can imagine the apostles' conversation upon meeting Paul after his conversion: "Well, I don't like this Paul fellow. Isn't his real name Saul? But I really like Barnabas."

Paul liked to be liked, too. Paul's ache to be liked, to be accepted in both his personality and ministry, is clearly evident in his epistles, such as 2 Corinthians. Yet even there, we see that all such desire was secondary to the message of the gospel and the work of the Holy Spirit.

"But the Jews stirred up the devout and prominent women and the chief men of the city, raised up persecution against Paul and Barnabas, and expelled them from their region. But they shook off the dust from their feet against them, and came to Iconium. And the disciples were filled with joy and with the Holy Spirit" (Acts

13:50-52, NKJV).

Some in Antioch of Pisidia really, really liked Paul and Barnabas; in fact, they owed their very lives to them. Others despised Paul and Barnabas; and really, who couldn't like Barnabas?

Maybe you know something of this, too. Where there's plenty of favor on your life—enjoy! It is a gift of God. And where there's relational struggle, ask yourself this question: "Is it due to my obedience to the Holy Spirit?"

If so, all desire to be liked is yielded to the leadership of God. If not, well, that's for another devotional about forgiveness and humility. May you be filled with joy and with the Holy Spirit!

*–Chris Manginelli, senior pastor of Mill Creek Foursquare Church in Lynnwood, Wash.*

### Discussion Points:

1. Have you ever found yourself on the losing end of an unexpected popularity contest and wishing you were liked more? Describe what happened.

2. In what ways does the popularity dilemma creep into our ministries and interfere with our effectiveness?

3. Describe the way the Apostle Paul dealt with the popularity dilemma.

### Prayer Points:

- Lord, be my affirmation, especially when others don't seem to like me very much.

- Shine a light on my life to show me where I am too concerned about my own popularity.

- Fill me, Holy Spirit, with Your joy, knowing that I do everything for You and Your Kingdom.

# ACTS 13: SHOW UP, STAND UP, SPEAK UP

BY GLENN BURRIS JR.

You've got to love Acts 13, where Paul told the Jews their own story. God selected them. They were a despised people, held in slavery, abused and forsaken. But in the middle of their journey, God rescued them and raised them up for a divine purpose. He made them a promise, and then He fulfilled it.

Although they conquered seven nations after crossing Jordan to possess the land, they were once again slaves, this time of the Roman Empire. God responded by depositing a Savior in their midst, whom they rejected.

A key verse for me is found in Acts 13:47, where Paul reminded the Jews that God made them "a light to the gentiles, that you should be for salvation to the ends of the earth" (NKJV).

We all know people who search their whole lives for clarity of purpose, a mission statement, something that will compel them with passion toward an end goal. Well, here it is. You would think they would jump on it. You would imagine that they would give up everything to get back on track to pursue the purpose for which they had been created.

Not so fast. We face the same struggles the Jews did. In the end, it really comes down to the pursuit of God versus the predictability of man.

Life is a constant struggle between God's plan and the devil's schemes. Even in heaven, Lucifer had another option, and a third of the angels were deceived. Though the Lord has spoken His Word over us, we often yield to another voice. In the midst of the struggle, we often lose our own voice and the influence that goes with it.

No one succeeds who has tried to serve two masters.

I was recently watching an episode of the CBS news program *60 Minutes* about Broadway producer Vy Higgensen, who runs a nonprofit ministry called "Vy Higgensen's School for Gospel, Jazz and RnB Arts." During the year that CBS correspondent Leslie Stahl followed this story, she discovered that Vy targets African-American teens in the five boroughs of New York City.

Vy had watched as a set of fast-paced and often tragic circumstances robbed these kids of their potential. In response, she is responsible for rescuing hundreds of kids who had become so trapped in the world around them that they had lost their way.

After screening them through auditions, Vy spends nine months molding the students into a dynamic choir of confident young people who reclaim their voice and rediscover their purpose. Watching the program, I was inspired by the radical change in their confidence in just one year.

Life's circumstances often rob people of the original voice they have been given. Sometimes our voice becomes muted, and the sound is indistinguishable.

In almost every recent article about the church in the Western world, an alarm has been sounded. Statistical analysis suggests that without some kind of intervention, the church will drift into oblivion. The favor that the church enjoyed in the past has become threatened. That voice of influence is often drowned out in myriad other sounds.

However, I am convinced that we can reclaim our voice. But it won't happen unless we use it.

Speak. Communicate in a way that others can understand! Sin, shame, spiritual sickness and solitude are clearly evident when our voice has become muted. But, there are at least four pathways that lead back to a place of influence: compassion, courage, character and competency.

Paul boldly reminded those who believed that God had clearly defined their destiny. When they embraced that destiny, "the Word of the Lord spread through the whole region" (v. 49).

Let's speak and reclaim our voice. The destiny of many people depends on it!

"Let your light so shine before men, that they may see your good works and glorify your Father in heaven" (Matt. 5:16, NKJV).

*–Glenn Burris Jr., president of The Foursquare Church.*

### Discussion Points:

1. In what ways has the church's voice become muted and indistinguishable among the noise of the world?

2. Identify one way that the church today can reclaim its voice.

3. How do you speak up in a way that others can understand?

**Prayer Points:**

- I want to serve only You, Lord; help me not to become sidetracked.

- As I determine to stand up for You, help me also regain my voice in this culture.

- I believe You have already determined my destiny; now, help me claim it.

# ACTS 13: LEADERS JUST LIKE US

BY LOUIE D. LOCKE

"Now in the church that was at Antioch there were certain prophets and teachers: Barnabas, Simeon who was called Niger, Lucius of Cyrene, Manaen who had been brought up with Herod the tetrarch, and Saul. As they ministered to the Lord and fasted, the Holy Spirit said, "Now separate to Me Barnabas and Saul for the work to which I have called them." Then, having fasted and prayed, and laid hands on them, they sent them away. So, being sent out by the Holy Spirit, they went down to Seleucia, and from there they sailed to Cyprus" (Acts 13:1-4, NKJV).

What stands out the most to me from this passage is the active, empowering, inspiring work of the Holy Spirit in the life of the church.

"The Holy Spirit said…"

"So, being sent out by the Holy Spirit…"

I think it's easy to look at the lives of Paul and Barnabas, these apostolic leaders and great men of faith, and to forget the fact that they were people just like us. They were called, gifted, strengthened and sent by the same Holy Spirit who is alive and at work in us.

The enemy of our souls, the devil, works hard in trying to make us feel alone. Insignificant. Forgotten. Left out of any important or worthwhile plans God has. He attempts to get us to focus on, compare and even covet the gifts, calling and missions of others. If he can do that, we end up distracted from our own mission, something that the Lord has called (and the Holy Spirit empowered) us to do and live out.

I'm praying today for a strong sense of divine purpose and calling—that we would not grow weary of doing good, that we'd live set apart to the Lord, that we would seek His face and hear the Holy Spirit-breathed directions for our lives.

*—Louie D. Locke, senior pastor of Fountainhead Foursquare Church in Carson City, Nev.*

### Discussion Points:

1. In what ways do you think your life is like the lives of Paul and Barnabas? In what ways is your life different?

2. When was the last time the enemy tried to attack you or your calling? What did you do, and how did things turn out?

3. How has the Holy Spirit recently reaffirmed His call in your life?

### Prayer Points:

▸ Spirit of God, remind me that You are always with me.

▸ When I feel alone and think I'm in a place that "no one has ever been," show me the cloud of witnesses who have gone before me and cheer for my success in Christ.

▸ Help me resist the enemy when he speaks lies about my life and ministry.

# ACTS 14

*"THE BILLIONS OF PEOPLE WHO HAVE YET TO RESPOND TO THE GOSPEL NEED A CHURCH THAT IS LESS CONCERNED WITH COMFORT AND MORE WILLING TO CONFRONT INJUSTICE AND SIN."*
*—GLENN BURRIS JR.*

# ACTS 14: CONFRONTING COMFORT AND COMPLACENCY

BY GLENN BURRIS JR.

James was his middle name, and he was a young Irish missionary committed to following the call of the Lord wherever it took him.

His fervor led him to Europe and then to Asia where, at 29 years of age, he contracted malaria and died on August 19, 1910. I visited his grave recently in an open cemetery that is filled disproportionately with military personnel who died in multiple wars and conflicts.

On his marble tombstone is a simple quote: "He led me to Christ." Aimee Semple McPherson stated those words. She had come to the Lord through the ministry of Robert James Semple, who would later become her husband and then ask her to follow him to Hong Kong.

Not long after arriving in Asia, he died, and just a little over a month later, Aimee would give birth to their daughter, Roberta. Now as a single mother, her journey would eventually lead her back to the United States, where she would found Angelus Temple and The Foursquare Church.

In our 21st-century view of the church, it's easy to forget about the extreme sacrifices that so many people have made and are making around the world for the sake of the gospel. I'm awed by the tenacity of so many who lead in the face of adversity and not only have persevered, but also have witnessed an explosion of God's favor and grace in the midst of trial and tribulation.

This morning, I sit only a short train ride away from China and realize that every day believers are making choices about their freedom or their faith. Sometimes I wonder if we in the West have gone a little soft in our faith. I find myself complaining about trivial things, and from time to time the Holy Spirit confronts me concerning my attitude.

Paul and Barnabas faced conspiracy, abuse and stoning, as recorded in Acts 14. They considered it a worthy price to pay for taking the gospel to the gentiles. Rather than disciple others on how to avoid it, they taught them that they should expect it.

The clarity of their message in Acts 14:22 declares, strengthening the souls of the disciples, exhorting them to continue in the faith, and saying, "We must go through many hardships to enter the kingdom of God." I wonder what grace and favor we may be missing when we devote so much time avoiding confrontation and adversity to make life more comfortable. My prayer is changing from "keep me safe" to "make me strong."

The billions of people who have yet to respond to the gospel need a church that is less concerned with comfort and more willing to confront injustice and sin. I have a renewed commitment to fill my life not with random activity, but with a clear purpose. This commitment includes a determined will to make a difference with my family, with my neighbors, with kingdom partnerships and with a world desperate to connect with the truth that will set them free.

*–Glenn Burris Jr., president of The Foursquare Church.*

### Discussion Points:

1. How has the Holy Spirit recently confronted you about your personal complacency?

2. In what ways does your teaching disciple people away from personal comfort and toward the real spiritual need around them?

3. Respond to this statement: "My prayer is changing from 'keep me safe' to 'make me strong.'"

**Prayer Points:**

- Rather than avoid difficulty, Lord, teach me to trust you even more in the face of adversity.

- Strengthen and deepen my faith in You, even if that means upsetting my personal comfort.

- Shake up my complacency, and equip me to take the love of Christ to the world.

# ACTS 14: IN PURSUIT OF OUR CALLING

BY TIM CLARK

"Now it happened in Iconium that they went together to the synagogue of the Jews, and so spoke that a great multitude both of the Jews and of the Greeks believed. But the unbelieving Jews stirred up the gentiles and poisoned their minds against the brethren. Therefore they stayed there a long time, speaking boldly in the Lord, who was bearing witness to the word of His grace, granting signs and wonders to be done by their hands.

But the multitude of the city was divided: part sided with the Jews, and part with the apostles. And when a violent attempt was made by both the gentiles and Jews, with their rulers, to abuse and stone them, they became aware of it and fled to Lystra and Derbe, cities of Lycaonia, and to the surrounding region. And they were preaching the gospel there" (Acts 14:1-7, NKJV).

Here are Paul and Barnabas, preaching boldly, being radically effective and moving powerfully in the Holy Spirit.

But the people of the city, both Jews and gentiles, were divided, and were against them.

This often happens when we are making an impact. People will be divided. The enemy doesn't like effective proclamation of the gospel, so opposition will come our way; resistance is to be expected.

What I didn't expect here is the response of these two—they ran away.

Sometimes we are supposed to die on the hill on which we are standing, like Stephen did in Acts 7. But other times it's OK to live to fight another day. Though it shocks me that bold Paul and Barnabas flee from the evil plans of their opponents, their flight doesn't seem to faze them. They just continue to preach the gospel in another location.

Maybe sometimes we get too wrapped up in our own plans and in our perception of how we are making an impact. Though faithfulness and stability are really good things, and much of our growth happens through challenging situations, if the context in which we are serving is killing us, perhaps there is not always dishonor in transition.

Anywhere we go there are people to be served and loved. The gospel needs to be carried everywhere, and unless we are disobeying a direct order from the Lord, getting out of harm's way just might be one of the possible methods God could use to get us where we need to be.

Remember, Jesus' command to "go make disciples of all nations" in Matt. 28 reads something like "as you are going and wherever you go, make disciples of all kinds of people and people groups." Since the implication is that we will already be going; maybe our calling isn't always as much to a particular place as it is to a purposeful pursuit wherever we happen to be.

Most times, it's probably some of both.

*–Tim Clark, district supervisor of the Greater Los Angeles District*

### Discussion Points:

1. How do you know the time is right to run from opposition like the apostles did in Acts 14?

2. Does the Holy Spirit ever require a person to remain in harm's way for the sake of the gospel? Explain why or why not?

3. In what ways do you understand your calling in light of "purposeful pursuit" as explained in this devotional?

### Prayer Points:

▸ What seems correct to me may oppose what You want me to do, Lord. Help me know what's right to do.

▸ If I should stand, infuse me with spiritual fortitude; if I should leave, give me the grace to run.

▸ Make an impact on the world through Your people, and help us get in and get out as You lead us.

# ACTS 14: SETTING MY EYES ON CHRIST

BY LOUIE D. LOCKE

"Then Jews from Antioch and Iconium came there; and having persuaded the multitudes, they stoned Paul and dragged him out of the city, supposing him to be dead. However, when the disciples gathered around him, he rose up and went into the city. And the next day he departed with Barnabas to Derbe.

"And when they had preached the gospel to that city and made many disciples, they returned to Lystra, Iconium, and Antioch, strengthening the souls of the disciples, exhorting them to continue in the faith, and saying, "We must through many tribulations enter the kingdom of God"
(Acts 14:19-22, NKJV).

Paul suffered violent opposition, persecution, slander and threat of death for his persistence in declaring the gospel. In Lystra, the mobs that had been chasing him from town to town finally caught up with him, dragged him out of the city, and stoned him until he was dead. Or at least they thought he was.

Whether he was resurrected from the dead or somehow had "shaken off" the stoning and recovered enough to walk we don't know. And just how might one "shake off" being pelted with rocks as big as your head? What we do know is that Paul got up, and moved on to the next city, Derbe, continuing to preach the gospel to any and all who would hear it. If that wasn't enough, Paul and Barnabas soon went back to Lystra, Iconium and Antioch of Pisidia, all places that angry hordes had either wanted to or attempted to kill them. And the message they preached was the Good News, and this good news and following Christ was worth every bit of suffering and hardship that would come, something they all knew Paul had experienced firsthand.

It makes me think about the confidence that Paul placed in his relationship with God, and how much he depended on the power of the Holy Spirit to sustain him through a life of such physical difficulty and suffering. What's more, he chose to set his mind on Christ, the author and finisher of our faith, so that he might be steadfast, firm in his pursuit of the goal and the mission he'd been given: that all would hear and come to know Christ, our hope and glory.

When Paul challenged the disciples in each city he visited to stand firm in their faith, to boldly persevere in the face of suffering, he spoke from experience. He had discovered the very real peace of God that goes beyond circumstances and had fully committed himself to the fact that God would sustain him until such a time that he died or was martyred. And this death—and even the threat of it—had no power or sway on him, for long before, he had chosen that whether he lived or died, it would be for the glory of God.

I pray for a fresh filling with the Holy Spirit for each of us. For boldness to live and declare the Good News without fear of what may come. And I set my eyes on Christ, purpose to follow in His footsteps and encourage others to do the same after me.

*–Louie D. Locke, senior pastor of Fountainhead Foursquare Church in Carson City, Nev.*

**Discussion Points:**

1. Is your relationship with God strong enough to withstand personal attacks like Paul experienced?

2. What changes is the Holy Spirit calling you to so you are equipped to fully stand for God?

3. What specific steps is God asking you to take to completely set your eyes on Him?

**Prayer Points:**

▸ I set my eyes on You, Jesus; help me see You in all Your glory and fullness.

▸ Fill me, Holy Spirit, and transform my vision that I will see as You see the world.

▸ Take fear far from me, and in its place give me a holy boldness as I share the things of God with the world.

# ACTS 15

*"WE ARE AFRAID GOD WON'T BE ABLE TO BE GOD IF WE DON'T HELP HIM."*
*—RON PINKSTON*

# ACTS 14-15: GIVING GOD THE GLORY

BY ALEX PACHECO

In Acts 15, Peter, Barnabas and Paul told of the wonderful things they had experienced in the name of the Lord, and those present listened intently. Then, James stood up and took his turn. He reminded them that Peter had already told them of God's plan to visit the gentiles, and also that the prophets of old had predicted this would happen.

"Then all the multitude kept silent and listened to Barnabas and Paul declaring how many miracles and wonders God had worked through them among the gentiles. And after they had become silent, James answered, saying, "Men and brethren, listen to me: Simon has declared how God at the first visited the gentiles to take out of them a people for His name. And with this the words of the prophets agree, just as it is written: 'After this I will return and will rebuild the tabernacle of David, which has fallen down; I will rebuild its ruins, and I will set it up; so that the rest of mankind may seek the Lord, even all the gentiles who are called by My name, says the Lord who does all these things.' Known to God from eternity are all His works" (Acts 15:12-18, NKJV).

These apostles prove to be good examples for us, as they declared what God did through them. They made sure to give God the glory for what He was doing. I believe what Jesus is showing me in this passage is that God's Word will come to pass. When it does, I cannot and should not take the credit for it.

I would be first to admit a tendency to leave God out of the picture; especially when I do something wonderful and I want a pat on the back. I may not do it on purpose, but somehow I forget to give Him the credit for all that I do in His name.

I know that the longer we do church, the easier it is to think this way. But, in reality, I'm so far from knowing it all. His Word is the ultimate test of truth, and we should always evaluate what we do in His name according to what is written in His Word.

"Lord, thank you for gently showing me that it's not about me. Please forgive me for the many times I've taken the credit and left You out by not saying anything about You. You are the one who does the miracles. It's all about You. I'm so glad You chose me and still love me, no matter what. Amen."

*–Alex Pacheco, district supervisor of Foursquare's Hawaii District.*

### Discussion Points:

1. Why is it so difficult to give God the glory when successes happen in the church?

2. In what ways do you remind yourself to pass along the glory to God?

3. How can you instill the truth about giving God all the glory in those you disciple?

### Prayer Points:

➤ Your Word is powerful and alive, and I believe You will accomplish it in my life.

➤ Use me, Lord, to touch the lives of others with the power of Your Spirit.

➤ When You work through me, I promise to quickly and completely give You the credit.

# ACTS 15: LEARNING NOT TO OUT-GOD GOD

BY RON PINKSTON

"'So why are you now trying to out-god God, loading these new believers down with rules that crushed our ancestors and crushed us, too?'" (Acts 15:10-11, The Message).

This is one of the questions of the ages. It's one the church has often answered poorly through the centuries. We are still very adept at piling things onto people. We pile on rules. We pile on our preferred daily disciplines. We pile on expectations for service … and so on and so on.

If we examine the motivation for all that piling on, it does tend to come down on the side of *out-godding* God. We're sometimes afraid, like the Pharisees were, that if we don't give the masses something to do they might leave us for someone who will. We are afraid God won't be able to be God if we don't help Him.

The spirit of the Pharisee is still roaming the religious corridors of time, seeking vulnerable people—people who will easily succumb to legalistic standards, and people who will partner in oppressing the freedom we've been given in Christ. All it takes is a little fear on the part of a leader, a little power based out of position, a little misplaced submission.

The Council at Jerusalem wrestled this question through to the Holy Spirit's conclusion. The danger for us comes when we stop wrestling and acquiesce to the demands of religion. Without that wrestling, we are like cars with our wheels out of alignment. We will gravitate toward placing burdens on people. It's what churches do. Let's trust the Lord of the church with His own people. He's up to the job.

"Jesus, help us to set people free from the burdens of religious life. Empower us to trust you with their souls. Keep us wrestling with the balance between legalism and license so we keep coming to the Holy Spirit's conclusions. In Your name, amen!"

*–Ron Pinkston, Central Pacific District supervisor.*

### Discussion Points:

1. How do you personally balance the tension between legalism and license?

2. Respond to this statement: "We're afraid God won't be able to be God if we don't help Him."

3. What would it look like in your ministry if God was truly, completely in control?

### Prayer Points:

➤ As I back off and let you be God in my life, please show me Your power and love.

➤ Transform my natural tendency to influence people so they truly follow you alone, Lord.

➤ Empower me to trust You for Your people; I believe You are up to the task.

# ACTS 15: STAYING FOCUSED ON THE MAIN THING

BY LOUIE D. LOCKE

"Now therefore, why do you test God by putting a yoke on the neck of the disciples which neither our fathers nor we were able to bear? But we believe that through the grace of the Lord Jesus Christ we shall be saved in the same manner as they" (Acts 15:10-11, NKJV).

Acts 15 tells of a crisis in the church; the number of believers in Christ was growing daily, and not just among Jews anymore. Now, even the gentiles were coming to Christ! So what was the crisis?

Certain groups among the Jewish believers couldn't imagine God calling and saving people who weren't circumcised. After all, circumcision was very significant for the Jew, as it marked the establishment of his covenant identity with God. Circumcision marked them in the most intimate way as a separate, distinct, people who belonged to the Lord.

I thank God for Paul, Barnabas and the Jerusalem council; when confronted with the pressing question, "What are we going to do about this?" they reminded their Christian brothers that the gospel being preached is one of grace and justification through faith. I imagine their debate with those who were demanding circumcision, wondering out loud what other hoops to jump through could have arisen if Paul and the others had given in. Dietary restrictions? Hair and beards? Rejection of one's culture of origin to embrace the Jewish culture?

Here we are, 2000-plus years later, mostly gentiles reading this, wondering what the big deal was. In hindsight it's easy to point out the Old Testament scriptures where God calls for the "inner circumcision," a circumcision of the heart. It's silly, because we know that we'd never put stumbling blocks in front of new believers, and for sure would never add to the gospel…would we?

I remember as a kid seeing people "different" from my family and me coming to church. I know now that they were "hippies"—

identified by their bare feet, old Levis, t-shirts, and mostly unkempt hair and beards. They really stood out.

I remember it was a big deal when they came to Christ, gave their testimonies of deliverance and expressed earnest desires for freedom from drugs or immorality, and to be clean and whole, and experience real love. I remember the discussions that took place where church leaders wrestled with the influx of new people, and wondered how we could help disciple them.

One suggestion rings in my ears: "What they really need is some different clothes and a haircut. They need to know that they're the temple of the Holy Spirit."

*Ouch.* We do this, too.

It makes me wonder: am I adding to the "main thing" of the gospel? Are there "Louie-isms" that are being elevated to "gotta do's"?

Lord, remind us that we are saved by Your grace, just as our brothers and sisters around the world are. Keep us sensitive to and focused on the Main Thing.

*–Louie D. Locke, senior pastor of Fountainhead Foursquare Church in Carson City, Nev.*

### Discussion Points:

1. What do you define as the "main thing" in your walk with Christ?

2. Describe ways you have struggled to remain focused on that "main thing."

3. How can you help others remain focused on the "main thing" as they disciple new Christians?

### Prayer Points:

▶ Lord, guard my heart so I don't require others to "do my will" in order to be saved.

▶ Show me any stumbling stones that I may put in front of people, and help me clear the path to You.

▶ Focus my heart, my mind, and my will on the Main Thing—Jesus.

# ACTS 16

*"WHEN WE ARE OBEDIENT TO THE VOICE OF THE HOLY SPIRIT AND WE CHOOSE TO PLACE VALUE ON WHAT HE VALUES, THE EARTH SHAKES, DOORS ARE OPENED, AND THE KINGDOM OF GOD PREVAILS."*
*—STEPHENIE MADSEN*

# ACTS 16: WHEN GOD SAYS "NO"

BY TAMMY DUNAHOO

Communication is an interesting matter. We all see and hear through a filter that has been shaped by our life events and how we have processed them. Our filters often like to hear "yes," and we can even tolerate "wait," as long as that wait is short-term. But we aren't fond of the word "no" from God. In fact, when we hear "no," we tend to believe it is the enemy blocking us, and so we muster our faith to rebuke the resistance.

In reality, it may be the "wind" of the Holy Spirit—that metaphor so often used to describe God's presence and working in our lives—that is causing the resistance. I read a commentary on Acts 16 that described this passage like part of St. Patrick's benediction that says, "May the wind be always at your back."

This was true for Paul's second missionary journey as they started to nurture the believers: "So the churches were strengthened in the faith and grew daily in numbers" (Acts 16:5, NIV). In two instances, God says "no" to Paul regarding the direction he and his band of missionaries are about to take.

As we know, the wind can blow in some unexpected directions, as it did for this group. Though we don't know the method God used to speak "no," it was clear that they had been "kept by the Holy Spirit from preaching the word in the province of Asia" (v. 6). Then again, when they tried to enter Bithynia, "the Spirit of Jesus would not allow them to. So..." (vv. 7-8).

The wind was blowing against them in some manner, but they seemed to understand the "no" of God was simply a redirection. Notice the word "so" in Acts 16:8. It was their response to God's "no." They knew the change of the wind wasn't intended to cause them to stop moving, nor was it for them to press into the wind and go against it.

Paul and his team had also come to discern the difference between being tossed to and fro by the wind rather than being led by it.

"How does God guide his church to the right place for mission?

There will be 'closed' as well as 'open doors.' There will be guidance addressed to individuals as well as to the entire team. There will be guidance via circumstances, sometimes extraordinary, as well as through the use of reason in evaluating circumstances in the light of God's Word. And specific guidance will come only to those who are already on the road, living out their general obedience to the Great Commission. Being able to say, 'God sent me; I come with the wind at my back,' is a strong witness to one's hearers that one's message is from God and true," (IVP New Testament Commentary Series, published by InterVarsity Press).

Do you feel as if a strong wind is blowing against you? Listen for God's "no," and see if He isn't redirecting you. There may be people waiting for you in your "Macedonia" (see Acts 16:9-15).

*–Tammy Dunahoo, Foursquare vice president and general supervisor.*

### Discussion Points:

1. How do you react when God redirects your path or your ministry direction?

2. Respond to this statement: "They knew the change of the wind wasn't intended to cause them to stop moving, nor was it for them to press into the wind and go against it."

3. Explain how God answering "no" can bring health and wholeness to your ministry.

### Prayer Points:

► Lord, help me accurately discern when You are saying "no" and when you are saying "go."

► I need Your help knowing how to redirect if I think I hear You telling me "not now."

► Keep my heart from discouragement when I really want to hear "yes," but I hear "no" instead.

# ACTS 16: FACING UNFORESEEN DETOURS

BY STEPHENIE MADSEN

Paul's travel to Macedonia in Acts 16 was not a conventional missionary journey, but rather a string of divine appointments stitched together by the Holy Spirit.

Through obedience, Paul found himself on an alternative or unplanned route that brought him to seemingly insignificant people, places and moments. These detours led Paul into a dark prison cell, bound and beaten for obeying the Spirit's leading.

Having seen the unchanging faithfulness of God throughout his journey, Paul was able to set aside his own discomfort and remain attentive to God's eternal agenda. His yielding to kingdom purpose positioned him to be used by the hand of God in miraculous ways:

"Suddenly there was a great earthquake, so that the foundations of the prison were shaken; and immediately all the doors were opened and everyone's chains were loosed. And the keeper of the prison ... called for a light, ran in, and fell down trembling before Paul and Silas. And he brought them out and said, 'Sirs, what must I do to be saved?'" (Acts 16:26-30, NKJV).

A jailer—a brute, crass, militant prison guard—found the love and power of a life-giving Savior through two men who served a God who leaves the 99 to go after the one (see Matt. 18:12).

As followers of Christ, we, like Paul, will find ourselves being led by the Holy Spirit into seemingly insignificant or undesirable moments when the ministry isn't thriving, a person's heart is still hardened, or the daily tasks are still mundane. It's in these moments that we are offered a choice to extend our vision and recognize the capacity that God sees in simple encounters with those who desperately need to know how He feels about them.

The salvation of one jailer turned into the opportunity to witness a whole family finding Jesus, resulting in an unforeseeable, God-size result, outside of what the Bible tells us.

When we are obedient to the voice of the Holy Spirit and we choose to place value on what He values, the earth shakes, doors are opened, and the kingdom of God prevails.

*–Stephenie Madsen, an Emerging Leader Network student who is part of Cascade Life Commission at Westside Church in Bend, Ore. She is the assistant to the pastor of Life Groups and is involved with Oneighty, her church's high school ministry.*

### Discussion Points:

1. How has your ministry pathway changed in recent months? Is God the cause of the detour?

2. In what ways have you, like Paul, been able to set aside your own discomfort and remain attentive to God's eternal agenda in the midst of an unforeseen detour?

3. What specific words of Scripture strengthen you during times such as this?

### Prayer Points:

▸ Lord, my circumstances sometimes seem like a prison, but I trust You to show me Your purpose in them.

▸ Use my life's detours to transform the lives of other people.

▸ I want to fully depend on the Holy Spirit to open doors and shake things up around me.

# ACTS 16: THE CHALLENGES OF A MATURE EXAMPLE

BY TIM CLARK

"Then he came to Derbe and Lystra. And behold, a certain disciple was there, named Timothy, the son of a certain Jewish woman who believed, but his father was Greek. He was well spoken of by the brethren who were at Lystra and Iconium. Paul wanted to have him go on with him. And he took him and circumcised him because of the Jews who were in that region, for they all knew that his father was Greek" (Acts 16:1-3, NKJV).

This is a strange event with even stranger timing.

Paul had just been sent by the apostles in Jerusalem to deliver to the gentiles the very exciting news that they didn't have to submit to Jewish customs and laws. This was exciting for many reasons, and one of the biggest ones for gentile men was that they wouldn't have to "go under the knife."

So, what gives here? Paul recruits a young man to accompany him on this journey where he would be delivering the incredible news of freedom and great relief that was decided by the church leaders, but he insists that Timothy is circumcised before joining him on this assignment.

Doesn't that seem hypocritical?

I used to think so, but as I've grown in leadership, I've come to understand there is a difference between setting a mature example and cowering before undue influence.

Sometimes you may have freedom to do something, but your gut tells you that your message will be more readily accepted if you forgo that freedom.

For instance, in Christ I'm certain I can dress how I want to in church without offending God, but if I'm speaking to a more conservative congregation, my ripped jeans and sneakers may immediately shut the ears of those who need to hear my message.

The point is that Paul was not willing to compromise what needed to be heard regarding the message of freedom by insisting on that very freedom for himself, or even his team. If you are on assignment at a church where you think the staff requirements are challenging, just be glad you weren't Timothy!

See, Timothy was half-Jewish, and if the Jews thought for a moment that Paul was trying to change Jewish religion and culture and not just extend this gospel he preached to the gentiles, they would go crazy trying to shut that message down—which is exactly what happened in Acts 21. Though that was a false accusation, Paul correctly understood the possible stakes for the message of the gospel. He did not see as hypocritical an action that might not reflect his own understanding of what is required for life in Christ (see Galatians), but that would clear the way for a helpful advance of his assignment.

Are we so insistent on our own rights that we declare as hypocritical any self-expression that may infringe on our freedom, or will we, like Paul, sometimes make painful but wise decisions to further the full message of grace?

*—Tim Clark, district supervisor of the Greater Los Angeles District.*

**Discussion Points:**

1. Describe a specific instance in your life when you gave up something so the faith of another person would be strengthened.

2. Have you ever seen this type of example in the life of another leader? What did it look like?

3. In what ways can a balanced, mature example result in developing healthy disciples for Christ?

**Prayer Points:**

► Remind me daily that my choices may influence the spiritual journey of others.

► Stimulate my heart to feel what others feel and see what others see.

► Help me always prioritize the furtherance of the gospel over my will or my preferences.

# ACTS 17

*"GOD IS TOO BIG FOR YOU TO HANDLE, MANIPULATE OR CONTROL. THIS IS GOOD NEWS AND BAD NEWS."*
—*DENNIS EASTER*

# ACTS 17: TURNING THE WORLD UPSIDE DOWN

BY JORDAN DECOSTA

We are skeptical of that which is foreign to us, and so our ministry is often inhibited by the challenge of presenting the gospel that so frequently seems to stand in sharp contrast to common worldviews. Paul encountered this deterrence as he reasoned with the people in Athens: "For you are bringing some strange things to our ears," they tell him, "therefore we want to know what these things mean" (Acts 17:20, NKJV).

This episode in Paul's life reminds us of what we sometimes forget: Our story is not only the greatest of stories; it is also universal. When the people of Athens thought he was preaching something strange, Paul brought his message back to their sphere of familiarity, telling the story from where they were. We do not serve a god who demands our ascent to His level by our own ability, but rather a God who "is not far from each one of us" (v. 27), so that if we seek Him, we will find Him.

In the context of our ministry, this reveals both a strategy for presentation and a reason for boldness. Paul demonstrated the strategy: He observed the city, recognized the points at which the Lord intersected their reality, and revealed to them that which they worshiped in ignorance.

Their reality conceived of a god, but they had no concept of One who did not exist in structures of their own design. Their reality told them that some higher power had created and ordered the world they knew, but it could not convince them that such a being might desire their hearts more than their service. Their reality assumed humanity had a source, but they could not imagine intimacy with a Creator.

Paul recognized these gaps in their reality and introduced the one true God and His exclusive gospel as their fulfillment. He simply told the story and extended the invitation to relationship in light of what he observed. Because he trusted that God would make

Himself real to his audience, Paul spoke with boldness—even in the face of a city's rejection.

We ought to keep Paul's strategy in mind in sharing the gospel. As we observe the lives of those God has called us to reach, He will provoke our spirits to recognize those points at which He can begin. We can then speak with boldness, trusting that He will move where His story is told.

And in doing so, we might again turn the world upside down.

*–Jordan DeCosta, a junior at Life Pacific College in San Dimas, Calif.*

### Discussion Points:

1. Have you ever "tried too hard" to convince someone of his or her need to be saved? What was the result?

2. What skill have you found is most important when trying to share the gospel with non-Christians?

3. In what specific ways does the Holy Spirit guide us to speak with relevance about His existence and His love for mankind?

### Prayer Points:

▶ Show me common ground from which I can begin to share the gospel with diverse groups of people.

▶ Help me trust You to draw people and to be ready to minister in Your name when I see them.

▶ Inspire me to speak boldly about Your goodness and the power of the Holy Spirit.

# ACTS 17: THE GOD WHO CAN BE KNOWN

BY DENNIS EASTER

Acts 17:22-23 says: "Then Paul stood in the midst of the Areopagus and said, 'Men of Athens, I perceive that in all things you are very religious; for as I was passing through and considering the objects of your worship, I even found an altar with this inscription: TO THE UNKNOWN GOD. Therefore, the One whom you worship without knowing, Him I proclaim to you'" (NKJV).

While Paul's presentation was for those who were seeking, it is a powerful reminder for us who have been found by God.

**God is the CREATOR of the universe:** "God, who made the world and everything in it, since He is Lord of heaven and earth, does not dwell in temples made with hands" (Acts 17:24).

God is too big for you to handle, manipulate or control. This is good news and bad news. The good news is that He is big enough to handle anything that concerns you. The bad news: If you think being in control of your destiny is the only way ... He is Lord as well.

**God is the SUSTAINER of life:** "Nor is He worshiped with men's hands, as though He needed anything, since He gives to all life, breath, and all things" (Acts 17:25).

God doesn't need anything from you except your needing of Him, and even that is for you.

**God is the RULER of all the nations:** "And He has made from one blood every nation of men to dwell on all the face of the earth, and has determined their preappointed times and the boundaries of their dwellings, so that they should seek the Lord, in the hope that they might grope for Him and find Him, though He is not far from each one of us; for in Him we live and move and have our being" (Acts 17:26-28a).

Where you find yourselves is not an accident with God. God has structured our lives in order to attract us to Him.

**God is the FATHER of human beings:** "…As also some of your own poets have said, 'For we are also His offspring.' Therefore, since we are the offspring of God, we ought not to think that the Divine Nature is like gold or silver or stone, something shaped by art and man's devising" (Acts 17:28b-29).

Idolatry is the attempt either to localize God or domesticate Him. The truth is, He is our Father, from whom we are meant to derive our very being.

**God is the JUDGE of the world:** "Truly, these times of ignorance God overlooked, but now commands all men everywhere to repent, because He has appointed a day on which He will judge the world in righteousness by the Man whom He has ordained. He has given assurance of this to all by raising Him from the dead" (Acts 17:30-31).

We are not moving toward some kind of personal extinction or some kind of absorption into Nirvana. Nope … we are heading toward a judgment encounter with God that will be universal, righteous and definite. We live as those who will someday give an account for their lives.

"Heavenly Father, in You we live and have our being. We humbly pray for You to guide and govern us, that in all the care and occupations of our lives, we may not forget You but remember that we are ever walking in Your sight. Through Jesus Christ our Lord, we pray. Amen."

*–Dennis Easter, district supervisor of Foursquare's Pacific Coast and Valleys District.*

### Discussion Points:

1. How is your faith strengthened knowing that God is too grand to manipulate but also close enough to live in you and be known by you?

2. Interact with this statement: "Idolatry is the attempt either to localize God or domesticate Him. The truth is, He is our Father, from whom we are meant to derive our very being."

3. What does it mean for Christians to live with the knowledge that we will one day give an account to God for how we lived our lives?

### Prayer Points:

- Keep my focus on You and Your plans for my life.

- Make me mindful that my situation is not an accident and that You are there with me.

- Guide and govern every part of my life, my ministry and my future.

# ACTS 18

# ACTS 18: EXPECTING SOMETHING MORE

BY TIM CLARK

"Now a certain Jew named Apollos, born at Alexandria, an eloquent man and mighty in the Scriptures, came to Ephesus. This man had been instructed in the way of the Lord; and being fervent in spirit, he spoke and taught accurately the things of the Lord, though he knew only the baptism of John. So he began to speak boldly in the synagogue. When Aquila and Priscilla heard him, they took him aside and explained to him the way of God more accurately" (Acts 18:24-26, NKJV).

The church today seems to be satisfied with the baptism of John. We leaders seek to be eloquent preachers, study hard to be competent in the Scriptures, are serious about being instructed (and instructing) in the way of the Lord, deeply develop ourselves to be spiritually fervent and are staunchly committed to speaking accurately concerning Jesus. We may speak and preach boldly, but we have to understand the way of God more accurately.

The fullness of the Holy Spirit seems to be a central theme in Acts. Disciples open up to God's transforming presence, and when the Holy Spirit flows through them, amazing things happen. I wonder if we have gotten too comfortable with our limited view of the way of God. We seem content to function in our own strength and relegate the Holy Spirit to the inner work, which produces fruit. Somewhere we have accepted the idea that the Holy Spirit doesn't work much supernaturally through us anymore.

Even Pentecostals (the tribe to which I belong) have backed off of our expectations. I remember one Sunday a friend of mine who was pastor at a Quaker church had a day off, and he came to visit my congregation. When we were chatting about his experience over coffee that week, he admitted that he was a little bit disappointed. He knew we were a Pentecostal church, and while he loved the service, he didn't find it much different than his own. He was expecting—and hoping for—something more!

So, why don't we have something more? Is it possible that even

Pentecostals have downplayed the supernatural expression of the Spirit and, in the process, have lost something important? I've often wondered if in the current missional conversations present in the body of Christ.

Those who have a developed theology and expressed experience in the life of the Spirit might have something important to offer.

Reread the book of Acts—and then read it again. It may create a hunger for you to embrace and engage the way of God more accurately in your ministry and life.

*–Tim Clark, district supervisor of the Greater Los Angeles District.*

### Discussion Points:

1. The same power from the book of Acts is available in our churches and ministries today; why is it we don't experience the same results?

2. Without going overboard trying to look particularly different from other evangelicals, what distinctive should we be known by as Pentecostals? What does that look like?

3. What can be done to develop a heart that is hungry for more of the Holy Spirit in your life and ministry?

### Prayer Points:

▸ Holy Spirit, fill me, transform me and use me for the purposes of Your Kingdom.

▸ If there are areas of my life where I am reluctant to welcome the Holy Spirit, challenge me, Lord, so You are fully welcome and at home there.

▸ Regardless how successful our ministries may be, remind us that we are nothing without the power of the Holy Spirit.

# ACTS 18: LIVING BETWEEN "NOW" AND "NOT YET"

BY ANDY OPIE

Reading Acts 18, I see suffering and struggle mixed with hope and victory. Paul's story is one of difficulty, emotion and upheaval intertwined with hope and joy. As a missionary who happens to be blind, I sit in the tension of struggle and victory as God uses me to touch others. In my life, I have seen God do incredible things, yet I still wait for him to heal me from blindness.

In Paul's life, we often miss the similar struggles that he had as we elevate him to immortal status as church-planter extraordinaire.

In Acts 18, Luke gives us insight into the humanity of Paul. We see him following similar patterns and coming away with similar results, and on the verge of throwing in the towel. This is when the Lord showed up to a despondent Paul in a vision during the quiet of the night.

Let's catch the back story before making some observations from Paul's vision.

Paul was in one of Greece's largest and most prosperous cities. As was his custom when entering the cities, he took the gospel to the Jews first by preaching at the synagogue. In turn, the Jews rejected Paul's preaching and abused him. Paul responded by shaking his cloak out at them. Paul then moved "next door" and took his message to the gentiles. It is in this backdrop that the Lord showed up to speak with Paul.

Luke left out the details as to what Paul was feeling, but we have some clues based on what the Lord said to him. First, because this was a vision and not a dream, Paul likely was up at night, agonizing over the repeated frustrations that buffeted him in preaching the gospel. Here are the four things Paul heard God say, as recorded in Acts 18:9-10 (NKJV); things that should encourage us in our context today:

1. "Do not be afraid," which all of us can relate to,

whether it is stepping out in new ministry or staying in a difficult place. We all have fears to which the Lord says, "Take courage."

2. "Speak, and do not keep silent," countering what is often the response of a fearful person. We easily stop speaking, because we wonder, "What is the use?" God encourages us to keep speaking, implying "don't give up."

3. "I am with you," hereby paralleling what Jesus said to His disciples at the Great Commission. We go because Jesus promised He would be with us. God did not promise easy roads ahead or untold numbers of miracles. He promised He would be with us. Our struggles and sufferings fade in the realization that Jesus is close to our side.

4. "No one will attack you to hurt you; for I have many people in this city." We can take courage, for as with Paul, God has people waiting in our cities to hear the message of the gospel and to be touched by His healing hand.

After receiving this vision from God, Paul stayed another 18 months, establishing one of the most dysfunctional churches in recorded history. God knew what was coming but still wanted this church to exist. This fact should give us great encouragement as we work within our local contexts!

We can take refuge in the realization that God reminded Paul that He was with him even in his turmoil. God knows where we are and what we are facing. He even knows the future problems that will come, but He asks us to persevere anyway.

In my story, I am constantly reminded by the Lord not to be afraid. I am encouraged not to give up on pressing in for my own healing. I have prayed for others and seen them healed, but why not me? I don't know the answer to that, but I know we sit in the tension between the "now" and "not yet" as the kingdom of God invades this world. As we stand in the assurance that God is with us, we can go in confidence to touch our cities with the love of Jesus.

*–Andy Opie, Foursquare missionary to Thailand.*

### Discussion Points:

1. What are you waiting on from the Lord, between "now" and "not yet"?

2. How have specific words from Scripture helped bolster your faith as you wait on God?

3. In what ways have you overcome fear during the waiting process?

### Prayer Points

▸ As I wait for You, Lord, build me up in the Holy Spirit and Your Word.

▸ Reveal what I should be doing for You while I wait for the "not yet" to come to pass.

▸ Prepare me to receive whatever You have in store for me, that I might pass on the blessing to others.

# ACTS 18: LIVING WHERE GOD DWELLS

BY TAMMY DUNAHOO

A few weeks ago, 25 Foursquare pastors and leaders followed the steps of Paul in Acts 18 as he left Athens and traveled to Corinth.

In Athens, we stood on Mars Hill in the shadow of the great Acropolis with its temples to pagan gods. We listened to Tim Clark (supervisor of the Greater Los Angeles District) and John Fehlen (senior pastor of West Salem Foursquare Church in Oregon) expound on the apostle Paul's words when he said: "'God ... does not dwell in temples made with hands'" (Acts 17:24, NKJV).

For the next several days, we traveled to Corinth, Patmos, Ephesus, Crete and Rome. We visited numerous cathedrals and basilicas built in honor of the apostles Paul, John and Peter. They were majestic, filled with gold and marble, and carefully crafted with artistic touches.

It was clear that no expense was spared all those centuries ago. But, in every temple and cathedral, I kept thinking about where God dwells.

On the last day of our tour, our final visit was to the catacombs. What a stark contrast this was to the ornate basilicas we had just encountered.

We walked underground, down four floors, and heard about the 500,000 people who were buried all around us. We passed by small rooms, some containing an altar denoting an area for worship.

We entered one of the rooms filled with the graves of an extended family, both adults and children. In this place deep inside the earth, and with awesome reverence, our voices rang out with the words of the doxology:

> *Praise God from Whom all blessings flow.*
> *Praise Him all creatures here below.*
> *Praise Him above, ye heavenly host.*

> *Praise Father, Son and Holy Ghost.*
> *Amen.*

As we sang, I have never felt such a profound sense of God's presence. The words of the great hymn hung in the air.

I was in awe of how many beautiful edifices we had walked through with crosses, symbols and altars of worship. Yet, in them all, I was left cold. But in this dark, dirt cave, I sensed the dwelling place of God. It wasn't because of the cave; it was because of the worship of our hearts, the place where God dwells.

I will never forget that experience!

As the apostle Paul came to Corinth, as was his practice he went to the synagogue to reason with the Jews. After being opposed and abused there, Acts 18:7 says, "And he departed from there and entered the house ... next door to the synagogue" (NKJV).

Our buildings are meant to be meeting places with God and His people. Whether a magnificent cathedral or an earthen cave, a synagogue or the house next door, God dwells in the hearts of the people who will worship Him there.

*–Tammy Dunahoo, vice president of U.S. operations, general supervisor.*

**Discussion Points:**

1. Interact with this Scripture: Acts 17:24: "God … does not dwell in temples made with hands."

2. Where do you go and in what setting do you most experience the profound presence of God? What makes the difference?

3. How can you as a leader help other Christians realize the powerful truth of God's abiding presence in their lives?

**Prayer Points:**

▸ I want to fellowship with You, Lord, and not be trapped by religious things.

▸ My heart is Your dwelling place; help me keep it pure for Your habitation.

▸ No matter how dark it may seem, I will depend on Your presence for my daily light.

# ACTS 18: LOOKING FOR THE HUNGRY BIRDS

BY LOUIE D. LOCKE

I'm amazed at how God can use the most mundane of life activities to bring people together. The apostle Paul left Athens and headed to the booming metropolis, and wide-open mission field, of Corinth. Left with the question of how he would support his gospel-spreading and church-planting campaign, Paul fell back on the trade he knew: tent making. And it just so happened that two members of the local tent-making guild were Aquila and Priscilla, a couple of refugees from Rome who had fled to Corinth at the order of Emperor Claudius because they were Christians. And, just like that, Paul had a team.

Paul followed his pattern of testifying to the Jews that Jesus is the Christ, His promised Anointed One. Here at Corinth, the message was soundly rejected, complete with threats of violence against Paul by the Jews. With the non-Jewish Corinthian audience, however, the response is drastically different. They believed. In large numbers, people in a city famous for sexual immorality and wild living flocked to the gospel of grace and the message of justification by faith.

Even though the Jews continued to threaten Paul, he knew that unlike Philippi, Berea and Thessalonica, he was to stick around Corinth for a while. The Lord Himself confirmed this, saying something to the effect of; "Keep it up. You won't be hurt. I've got lots of people here, and you've got lots to preach, teach, and train."

I often think about how the Apostle Paul wrestled through the dichotomy of the two responses to the gospel at Corinth, where one group soundly rejected and strongly opposed the Good News, and the other joyfully embraced and applied it. I think that this contradiction was at the forefront of his mind as he wrote letters back to Corinth:

"For the message of the cross is foolishness to those who are perishing, but to us who are being saved it is the power of God. For

Jews request a sign, and Greeks seek after wisdom; but we preach Christ crucified, to the Jews a stumbling block and to the Greeks foolishness, but to those who are called, both Jews and Greeks, Christ the power of God and the wisdom of God. Because the foolishness of God is wiser than men, and the weakness of God is stronger than men" (1 Cor. 1:18, 22-25, NKJV).

One way I like to think about this is that my role in sharing the gospel and investing in discipleship is "looking for the hungry bird." What I mean is this: when the mama bird comes back to her nest after a morning of worm-digging and bug-grubbing, the baby bird that gets to eat is the hungry one, the one with the open beak. In the same way, I want to be looking for the "hungry birds," those people who eagerly hear and respond to the Good News. This doesn't mean ignoring others, but rather is a picture of looking for where God is actively at work, and then intentionally partnering with the work He's already done in preparing the "soil'" of their hearts.

I pray that we would have eyes to see the hungry birds in our lives today.

–Louie D. Locke, senior pastor of Fountainhead Foursquare Church in Carson City, Nev.

**Discussion Points:**

1. Describe what the Lord has recently said to you about the struggles and successes of your ministry.

2. Does the "looking for hungry birds" concept resonate with you? Why or why not?

3. In what ways do you believe you are partnering with the Holy Spirit to reach people whose hearts have been prepared to receive the gospel?

**Prayer Points:**

▸ Give me eyes to see those in my life who are hungry for more of God.

▸ Equip me to help disciple people who are most willing to follow God.

▸ Fill me with Your grace to help reach those who aren't ready to fully partake of Your goodness.

# ACTS 19

*"THE BAPTISM OF THE HOLY SPIRIT FILLS US WITH THE POWER TO BE TRULY TRANSFORMED AND ABLE TO LIVE AS GOD'S FOREVER REDEEMED."*
*—BILL GROSS*

# ACTS 19: CONTENDING FOR UNUSUAL MIRACLES

BY LISA PENBERTHY

"Now God worked unusual miracles by the hands of Paul, so that even handkerchiefs or aprons were brought from his body to the sick, and the diseases left them and the evil spirits went out of them" (Acts 19:11-12, NKJV).

During a recent visit to the doctor, my 6-month-old son was diagnosed with a chromosomal deficiency. My heart immediately ached for my son's well-being, and while I would like to say my first instinct was to turn to God in prayer, the oh-so-human side of me surfaced with a multitude of questions. What does this mean? What will it look like in the long run?

After the list of "what" questions, the "why" questions began to take over. Why my son? Why this deficiency? Why? Why? Why?

I began to realize how negative the "why" questions were becoming, and knew that ultimately I was questioning God—who wonderfully and fearfully made my son. I began to take control over my thoughts and cry out to God. I reflected on the many promises of God for healing and the miracles that happened daily throughout the New Testament and still happen today.

Acts 19 says that after two years, Paul left Ephesus and "all who dwelt in Asia heard the word of the Lord Jesus" (v. 10). Paul spent much of his time there teaching and preaching, and moving in the power of God. It was in that power that was so real in his life that the evidence of "unusual miracles" was known. People took handkerchiefs and aprons from him to the sick so they would be healed.

I want to see that power at work in my son's life. It is the miraculous that I am contending for, and the testimony that will follow, so that all may hear the Word of the Lord. This is what we are called to do as believers and followers of Christ; this is what we were made to do as we reach the harvest.

I am contending for unusual miracles. Are you?

*–Lisa Penberthy, operations director for the Foursquare National Church Office.*

### Discussion Points:

1. Have you experienced God's unusual miracles in your life? Give an example.

2. Why do you think Acts 19 specifies that the miracles were "unusual"?

3. How open are you to pray for and expect God to perform unusual miracles in your ministry and in your home? What specific steps will you take to encourage others to believe with you?

**Prayer Points**

- When crises strike, help me to trust You fully and not to doubt You.

- I contend for the miraculous, Lord, and for Your touch in those around me.

- When You do unusual miracles, I will be faithful to share those with others.

# ACTS 19: TRANSFORMED LIVING IN HOLY SPIRIT FULLNESS

BY BILL GROSS

"Did you receive the Holy Spirit when you believed?" (Acts 19:2, NKJV).

I love the apostle Paul!

There, I said it. I love Paul's courage, his knowledge, his faithfulness, his passion for Jesus, his commitment to living every day as if his future depended on it. I love his confident faith in knowing that his future was secure in Christ.

I admire how Paul lived the gospel and walked in the Spirit—and most of all, I admire how he saw those two endeavors as a single action, inseparable both in missiology and practicality.

Clearly the apostle Paul believed that receiving the Holy Spirit was critical to living as a disciple of Jesus Christ.

I am not sure what Paul saw when he arrived in Ephesus that would have prompted such a penetrating question: "Did you receive the Holy Spirit when you believed?" Possibly these disciples were caught in the Old Covenant struggle of sin and repentance. They may have been valiantly applying their human determination as the spiritual weapon of choice to gain a victory that is only won by the transforming work of the Holy Spirit.

Whatever the reason, the apostle Paul asked the question that defines our unique place in the body of Christ. It is our powerful Foursquare belief that the baptism of the Holy Spirit is an amazing gift of God. We believe that the fullness of the Holy Spirit enables us to live beyond a conviction to repent and our human determination to never sin again.

The baptism of the Holy Spirit fills us with the power to be truly transformed and able to live as God's forever redeemed.

As modern-day Christians, will we forever strive to find better ways to do church, but miss our distinctive invitation to be the church?

Will we continue to search for more contemporary ways to deliver our message and more culturally authentic ways to live together in community? Or will we echo the compassionate and powerful words of the apostle Paul: "Did you receive the Holy Spirit when you believed?"

In the aftermath of such a great baptism, we will find the works of the Holy Spirit in our lives that we need to truly live the gospel of Jesus Christ.

"Let the Spirit be lacking, and there may be wisdom of words, but not the wisdom of God; the powers of oratory, but not the power of God; the demonstration of argument and the logic of the schools, but not the demonstration of the Holy Spirit" (Arthur T. Pierson, Presbyterian minister, 1837-1911).

*–Bill Gross, Foursquare missional development coach.*

### Discussion Points:

1. How important do you think the baptism with the Holy Spirit is? For yourself? For those you lead?

2. Describe the transformation that occurred in your life when you were baptized with the Holy Spirit.

3. Reflect on this statement: "We believe that the fullness of the Holy Spirit enables us to live beyond a conviction to repent and our human determination to never sin again."

### Prayer Points:

▸ Fill me with Your Holy Spirit, that I will live a transformed life.

▸ Keep my focus on the deep truth of Spirit-transformed living and not merely on trends.

▸ Give me Your wisdom and not just clever words, Lord.

# ACTS 19: UPSETTING THE STATUS QUO

BY TIM CLARK

"For you have brought these men here who are neither robbers of temples nor blasphemers of your goddess" (Acts 19:37, NKJV).

Paul had obviously upset the order of things in Ephesus. He was proclaiming a message that caused people to turn from their twisted worship, and the ministry was so successful that many abruptly stopped participating in occult practices and ceased supporting the local idol trade. Because this was more than a handful of Christians boycotting the industry, there was serious concern among those who made their living from selling religious workmanship.

So they were rioting, and were ready to tear Paul and company limb from limb to save their industry, but cooler heads prevailed.

What amazes me is the reason for these cooler heads. The city clerk correctly reminded these people that at no time during the preaching of Paul's message did he rip them off or even blaspheme their primary deity.

That always gives me pause.

And I ask myself, "Is there a way to preach the Good News of Jesus without having to actively go after and brutally rip apart other people's belief systems first?"

Sometimes I wonder if the gospel itself is a weapon that demolishes the strongholds and pretensions that set themselves up against God, and I wonder if we should focus more on simply and boldly preaching the true gospel.

Because part of this gospel is that Jesus alone is Lord. There is a choice that must be made between Him and other objects of worship. But maybe we don't have to go on the offensive like a cheap political-campaign strategist, trying to find the dirt on all the other "god-candidates." Perhaps the proper exaltation of the one true God and the explanation that He will not share His glory with any other is often enough to diminish not only false worship, but all of the structures that support that worship as well.

Please hear me: I'm not suggesting that proper apologetics or exposing destructive objects of worship does not have its place, but that sometimes a Spirit-empowered preaching of the gospel "can bring freedom from bondage without us having to set up a website declaring ourselves as the "blasphemers" of what others are worshiping.

*–Tim Clark, district supervisor of the Greater Los Angeles District.*

### Discussion Points:

1. What would happen in your town if Christians focused exclusively on the good news of salvation rather than on fighting and tearing down each other's doctrine?

2. In what ways do you think the gospel itself and the exaltation of the one true God would dispel all other false teachings?

3. What part of this process is tied up in our genuine ability to love people as Jesus loves them?

### Prayer Points:

➤ When I am tempted to attack the beliefs of others, remind me that the gospel only needs to be shared, not defended.

➤ As I praise You for Your greatness, help others begin to see the value of following You.

➤ Make me a contagious Christian so that I can help spread Your love to a dying world.

# ACTS 20

*"WE ARE CALLED TO DO MORE THAN PREACH SUPERFICIAL MESSAGES THAT TEMPORARILY QUENCH HUNGER. INSTEAD, WE SHOULD DECLARE THE ENTIRE COUNSEL OF GOD THAT NOT ONLY SATISFIES, BUT ALSO NOURISHES."*
*—MARCUS ELLINGTON*

# ACTS 20: CHAINS AND TRIBULATIONS AWAIT ME

BY JIM SCOTT

Acts 20 makes a significant change in focus for Luke as he recounts the spread of the gospel from Jerusalem to the nations.

C. Peter Wagner comments that "in the remaining nine chapters of his book, Luke gives us very little additional information about missiology, church planting or power ministries ... concentrating more on Paul's experiences of being jailed and defending himself in courtroom-type scenes" (*The Acts of the Holy Spirit*, p. 490).

With this in mind, I was struck by Paul's address to the Ephesian elders in Miletus: "You know, from the first day that I came to Asia, in what manner I always lived among you, serving the Lord with all humility,with many tears and trials which happened to me. ... And see, now I go bound in the spirit to Jerusalem, not knowing the things that will happen to me there, except that the Holy Spirit testifies in every city, saying that chains and tribulations await me. But none of these things move me; nor do I count my life dear to myself, so that I may finish my race with joy, and the ministry which I received from the Lord Jesus, to testify to the gospel of the grace of God.  And indeed, now I know that you all, among whom I have gone preaching the kingdom of God, will see my face no more" (Acts 20:18-25, NKJV).

The Comforter, the Holy Spirit, promised jail and suffering to Paul, and he embraced it as certainly as one would accept any promise from God. And this was not a unique or momentary season of trouble for Paul. In the apostle's very calling, Jesus promised that "[Paul] is a chosen vessel of Mine to bear My name before gentiles, kings and the children of Israel. For I will show him how many things he must suffer for My name's sake" (Acts 9:15-16).

Later, in his letter to the Philippians, Paul reminded his dear friends that they had "…been granted on behalf of Christ, not only to believe in Him, but also to suffer for His sake" (Phil. 1:29, NKJV).

It seems that there is a theology of suffering. The essence of theology—the study of God—is more than doctrine; as the Puritans taught, it is teaching that enables us to live for and serve God.

Suffering, in some extraordinary and mysterious way, enables us to live for God. And this life lived for God is powerful and transformational—even during a season such as when Paul confessed his suffering and weakness because of his "thorn in the flesh" (see 2 Cor. 12:1-8) while, at the same time, handkerchiefs and aprons that had touched his body were instrumental in healing people in Ephesus (see Acts 19:11-12). These extraordinary miracles give new meaning to his declaration, "For when I am weak, then I am strong" (2 Cor. 12:10).

I want to know more about this theology of suffering and the power that comes when I acknowledge that God is at work. I want to be able to embrace this mysterious work and serve my God who is glorified in weakness and in loss.

"Jesus, may the global and, in some places, the suffering Foursquare Church be a glory to You even as we suffer. May we all live confessing that our lives are worth nothing to us unless we use those lives for finishing the work of telling others the Good News about the wonderful grace of God."

*—Jim Scott, Foursquare vice president and director of Foursquare Missions International.*

### Discussion Points:

1. The Apostle Paul knew that suffering awaited him in almost every city, yet he followed the Holy Spirit there anyway. What parallels do you see between your ministry and that of Paul's?

2. In what ways does your life reflect this sentiment: "I want to be able to embrace this mysterious work and serve my God who is glorified in weakness and in loss."

3. What does 2 Cor. 12:10 mean to you in light of your weakness and God's strength?

### Prayer Points

- Lord of Comfort, prepare me to stand for You in every circumstance and for the glory of God.

- Help me receive every promise You have for me, even if it is a promise of suffering.

- Father, I will live my life with the realization that my life is worth nothing unless I tell others the Good News about the grace of God.

# ACTS 20: APPRECIATING THE SOFTER SIDE OF PAUL

BY JOHN FEHLEN

"And when he had said these things, he knelt down and prayed with them all. Then they all wept freely, and fell on Paul's neck and kissed him, sorrowing most of all for the words which he spoke, that they would see his face no more. And they accompanied him to the ship" (Acts 20:36-38, NKJV).

This might be one of the more tender passages in Scripture and an intimate glimpse into the apostle Paul that we don't often see. Basically, it's his softer side. Much of the time we follow Paul on his missionary journeys, teaching and preaching, working miracles, training and rebuking, and planting and shaping the direction of the fledgling church.

Here, however, he is weeping. Why? Because he loves the people of Ephesus.

Paul spent a handful of years with this congregation, more time than with any other group. He bonded. He grew with them. He was deeply concerned about their well-being, which was evident from the instructions he gave the Ephesian elders before departing to Jerusalem. He asked them to carefully watch over the congregation, to guard it from wolves with ill motives and to continue building up the church with the word of grace.

It's probably similar to a father giving away his daughter to the boy—I mean man—that she is marrying. With hopefully anticipation, and yet a wave of trepidation, one must trust that the hand-off will be successful.

Will the church/daughter be loved, cared for and nurtured?

These are the questions a father asks, if he has any semblance of a heart. This is what Paul is asking as well. All too often, we miss the heart of Paul because we tend to focus only on his firm corrections and doctrinal challenges. But, he had a softer side too.

I like the softer side of Paul. How about you?

–John Fehlen, pastor of West Salem Foursquare Church in Oregon.

**Discussion Points:**

1. Describe an experience in your ministry when you wept over the people you were leading.

2. What was the motivation behind Paul's instructions to the Ephesian elders in Acts 20?

3. How comfortable are you with allowing the tenderness of the Holy Spirit to show in your leadership?

**Prayer Points:**

- Put me in touch with the things that move Your heart, O God.

- Help me see others with Your eyes; help me identify with their concerns just the way You do.

- If any part of my heart is hard or resistant, soften me and use me more fully, Lord.

# ACTS 21

*"IF I'M LIVING A LIFE OF OBEDIENCE TO
THE LORD—LIVING FOR ETERNITY AND NOT
JUST FOR COMFORT IN THE HERE AND NOW—
I WILL SUFFER.  THE GOOD NEWS IS THAT
MY PRESENT SUFFERING WON'T COMPARE TO
THE GLORY THAT WILL BE REVEALED. . ."*
**—LOUIE D. LOCKE**

# ACTS 20-21: NOURISHING OUR SPIRITUAL APPETITES

BY MARCUS ELLINGTON

"For I have not shunned to declare to you the whole counsel of God" (Acts 20:27, NKJV).

In his farewell speech to the elders of the church of Ephesus, the apostle Paul thought it necessary to communicate the fact that he had fulfilled his duty among them. He had not held anything back, but instead declared to the people of Ephesus the entire counsel of God. He exhorted the elders with his own example of preaching a complete and balanced doctrine that eradicated any doubt or lack of knowledge.

As ministers of the gospel today, it is our responsibility to do the same. We must spiritually feed the flock, ensuring not only that are they fed, but also that they are nourished. Just as in the physical realm there are foods that quench the pangs of hunger but offer very little nourishment, some try to sustain their spiritual lives on "food" that may quiet the hunger pangs but does not spiritually nourish.

I believe the call of the Lord for us today is this: to declare the entire counsel of God. We are called to do more than preach superficial messages that temporarily quench hunger. Instead, we should declare the entire counsel of God that not only satisfies, but also nourishes.

In Luke 4, Jesus quoted from Deut. 8: " 'Man shall not live by bread alone, but by every word of God'" (v. 4). Physical food brings temporary rectification, but spiritual nourishment from the Word of God brings true nourishment and satisfaction.

I want to encourage all of us as ministers to not cower from declaring the entire counsel of God, even when it is unpopular to do so. May we, like Paul, recognize our extreme responsibility as shepherds and ensure that our words are His words that nourish and satisfy, producing eternal evidence and life more abundant.

*–Marcus Ellington, Southwest District NextGen director and senior pastor of Living Hope Christian Fellowship (Dana Point South Foursquare Church) in San Clemente, Calif.*

### Discussion Points:

1. How do you ensure that those you teach are truly being nourished in the Word of God?

2. What balance of spiritual nutrients do you include in your teaching ministry?

3. How do you define the "whole counsel" of God?

### Prayer Points:

▸ Help me prepare and deliver Your Word so it truly fills those who hear that word.

▸ Even when it's unpopular to do so, cause me to speak Your truth in power.

▸ Nourish me, Lord, so I can provide spiritual nourishment to others.

# ACTS 21: DETERMINED TO BE OBEDIENT

BY HARRIET MOUER

As Christians, we receive a lot of counsel from fellow believers, and most of that advice is intended for good. But what happens when our perceived direction from God clashes with others' advice? Sometimes we must choose to be obedient to what we feel God's leading for our life is, and pray others see that we are letting Him direct our paths.

After a spectacular chairlift ride atop Mt. Hermon in northern Israel, I met Susan and her Jewish family, who were vacationing from South Carolina. When Susan was a young teen, she made up her mind to serve in the Israeli army. To her father's dismay, she was trained to be on the front lines in combat duty. And no one could talk her out of what she felt was her life's God-ordained purpose.

Similarly, the apostle Paul was determined to be obedient to the Holy Spirit's leading even when those closest to him—including people he greatly respected and esteemed—warned him of dire consequences.

Acts 21 begins with Paul's journey to Jerusalem by sea, from Ephesus to Tyre in Syria, where he sought out the believers in that city. Paul's team stayed there for seven days, and in that time they grew to love their new missionary friend. "Through the Spirit," the believers told Paul not to go to Jerusalem, fearing for his safety (see v. 4). It was another emotional goodbye that included the children. (This is the first time children are mentioned in the apostolic church.)

Two days later, they came to Caesarea. Paul's host was Philip, the evangelist, and his four prophetic daughters, indeed a fulfillment of Joel 2:28. While at Philip's home, the prophet Agabus came from Judah. In a dramatic gesture, he took Paul's belt, which was a long piece of cloth that he could wrap around himself several times.

Tying himself up hands and feet, Agabus prophesied: "Thus says the Holy Spirit, 'So shall the Jews at Jerusalem bind the man who owns this belt, and deliver him into the hands of the gentiles' " (Acts 21:11, NKJV).

Again the believers repeatedly begged him not to go. They valued and loved him; however, they concluded their prophecies were a prohibition, not just a warning. Their hysteria didn't budge Paul. "What do you mean by weeping and breaking my heart? For I am ready not only to be bound, but also to die at Jerusalem for the name of the Lord Jesus," Paul insisted (v. 13).

Their response? Quietness! Stillness! Finally, they spoke: "The will of the Lord be done" (v. 14).

Like Paul's friends, do we draw conclusions for our friends and loved ones out of our own discernment?

Susan's dad had to come to grips with her serving in combat even though he did not like it. May we ask God to carry out His desire in our friends and loved ones, fulfilling His mission through them—even if we don't particularly like it. And may we say, "The will of the Lord be done."

*—Harriet Mouer, Mid-Atlantic district supervisor.*

### Discussion Points:

1. Sometimes it is easy to draw conclusions about what others should do from our own discernment and not from what God wants to say. Has this ever happened to you? Have you ever done this to others?

2. What understanding is necessary for us to completely trust God's leading even when others disagree?

3. When you speak prophetically over someone's life, how do you guard your heart so you know the word is from God?

**Prayer Points**

- Wipe away everything that might get in the way of me being fully obedient to Your plans.

- Fulfill Your mission through my friends and family— even if I don't particularly like it .

- In everything and in every life, my prayer is that Your will is done.

# ACTS 21: PURSUING GOD'S MISSION

BY LOUIE D. LOCKE

Acts 21 tells of Paul's intent to head to Jerusalem, and also the fact that he received several prophetic words and pictures declaring that if he went to Jerusalem he would be thrown into prison.

I never understood why, after hearing these multiple warnings from the Holy Spirit of the imprisonment, persecution and suffering awaiting him in Jerusalem, Paul still purposed to go to Jerusalem. I even tried to come up with possible reasons why he might be so intent to finish this journey; none of the reasons made sense, especially considering the man the apostle Paul was. So I asked the Lord, "What would make a man choose this path and persist in the face of what looks like preemptive warnings of danger and trouble from the Spirit?"

Immediately, an earlier portion of Paul's story flashed into my mind, from the time right around his conversion (Acts 9:10-19). From the beginning, God revealed that He had made Paul His "chosen instrument" (v.15) to testify of Christ and spread the gospel before the gentiles, kings and the children of Israel. And one of the first things revealed to Paul was how much he would suffer for the sake of the name of the Lord.

*Aha!* I get it. Paul was on a mission from God.

The single-minded purpose to get to Jerusalem wasn't an exercise of stubbornness on Paul's part—he simply understood that this was part of the living out of the mission given to him by the Lord years before. The fact that his obedience and persistence could (and would) result in imprisonment and suffering were almost an afterthought; the mission, and the spread of the gospel, were preeminent.

I think that we might have an underlying assumption that suffering is to be avoided at all costs, probably because suffering hurts. Digging deeper, we may have an unscriptural karma-like belief about good and bad happening in our lives; e.g., if we're doing what God wants us to do, life will be good, and if not, then that's when the bad stuff happens.

Jesus told His disciples, "A servant is not greater than his master. If they persecuted Me, they will also persecute you..." (John 15:20,

NKJV). If I'm living a life of obedience to the Lord—living for eternity and not just for comfort in the here and now—I will suffer. The good news is that my present suffering won't compare to the glory that will be revealed in, through, and around us in Christ Jesus and by His Spirit (Rom. 8:18).

Paul was sure about one thing: God had given him a mission, and therefore, whatever it took to complete the mission, he knew that God would provide it.

I pray for such a faith to grow in my heart and mind, and for that kind of faithful perseverance to the calling and mission that God has placed in front of me. Lord, help me live life with eternity and Your values firmly in sight, and with a single-minded focus on my mission.

*–Louie D. Locke, senior pastor of Fountainhead Foursquare Church in Carson City, Nev.*

### Discussion Points:

1. How clearly do you understand God's mission in your life and ministry? Are there fuzzy or confusing areas that still need clarification?
2. What areas of life challenge you and potentially distract you from fulfilling that mission?
3. How much help is it to you in your ministry when you read passages such as Rom. 8:18?

### Prayer Points:

- Clarify what Your mission is for my life and equip me to pursue that mission with all my strength.

- From beginning to end, I want my life to be completely consistent with Your mission for me.

- Help me stubbornly pursue Your mission for me even though life and circumstances may not always seem to go along with that plan.

# ACTS 21: KNOWING WHEN GOD SPEAKS

BY TIM CLARK

In Acts 21 there is a strange sequence of events that can make us wonder if Paul isn't paying attention to the word of the Lord. He is repeatedly met with opposition from his friends who are prophesying (correctly) that he will find nothing but heartache and pain if he completes his travel to Jerusalem.

Accompanying those prophecies are strong personal warnings against continuing his trip. Paul seems to smile, nod and then say, "Thanks, guys, but I'm going anyway." What does it mean?

I actually love this passage because it tells us some important things about prophetic words given to us today:

1.  The interpretation of the person doing the prophesying does not always sync up with the Spirit's prophetic intention. Have you ever seen it? God speaks through someone, and then that someone keeps on speaking long after God has stopped?

    It reminds me of the true story of a friend who was a first-time pastor in a congregation that was new to him. One lady stood up and declared, "Thus sayeth the Lord..." then proceeded to judgmentally lambaste the congregation over what was apparently horribly wrong with all of them. Everyone was silent wondering how the new, young pastor would respond. Before he could say anything, someone else stood up and boldly said, "Thus sayeth the Lord, I did not say that," and sat back down.

    This illustrates the fact that sometimes we hear incorrectly; other times we are right on target with what the Holy Spirit is saying, but we decide we also know exactly what the prophecy must mean. Many times the one prophesying is not supposed to "help

God out" and unpack the word; that is most often the responsibility of the hearer.

2. Prophecy is not meant to be a billy club to force us into actions that conflict with the direction we are sensing the Lord is taking us. Accountability is good, and we should listen to the advice of those close to us. However, demanding that the word of the Lord I give should require someone to do what I think they ought to do will quickly turn into spiritual coercion, or even abuse.

   Listen to prophetic words gratefully, and seek to understand the intent God has for you in giving that word.

3. To correctly interpret prophecy, we need to be viewing it through an eternal lens. Just because someone prophesies that something challenging is about to happen to you, it doesn't mean that God's intent is that you avoid that challenging situation. It may be the Lord preparing you to face it so that you can be shaped.

   Paul responded not with a reaction that would benefit him temporarily, but with an understanding of God's larger work in which he was involved.

Readily receive personal prophecy—as long as it doesn't contradict with what God has already revealed in His Word. Let it radically impact your life. But remember to test it (1 Thess. 5:19-21). Just because someone is speaking God's specific words to you, it doesn't mean that he or she is the mouthpiece of God for all that He has planned for your life.

*–Tim Clark, district supervisor of the Greater Los Angeles District.*

### Discussion Points:

1. How do you accurately spiritually discern the validity of a personal prophetic word?

2. Like Paul, have you had an experience where you chose to disregard a personal word and do something else instead? What happened?

3. To what extent are spiritual authority and accountability a factor in sharing and receiving personal words of prophecy?

**Prayer Points:**

- Sensitize me, Holy Spirit, so I will clearly know Your voice when You speak to me.

- Teach me to discern personal words of prophecy, Lord.

- Keep my heart soft so that I can gratefully receive direction and encouragement from Your Spirit.

# ACTS 22

*"CEASING TO BE GRATEFUL FOR GOD'S GRACE PRODUCES SELF-RIGHTEOUSNESS AND LEGALISM; DISREGARDING HIS VOICE CULTIVATES SPIRITUAL DEAFNESS, MAKING US VULNERABLE TO DECEPTION; AND DEMANDING CONFORMITY TO OUR MOLD REAPS AN OPPRESSED HARVEST."*
**—DAWN HOUK**

# ACTS 22: GIVING AWAY EXTRAVAGANT GRACE

BY DAWN HOUK

Throughout history, God has lovingly extended His grace to situations and people who do not fit the accepted, religious mold. In my life's journey I have encountered Christians who, for whatever reason, struggle or are unable to extend grace to others.

In contrast, I have met non-Christians who readily exhibit forgiveness and acceptance of others. How is this possible? How can we who have been forgiven ever refuse to extend God's grace to another? It is a painful grievance that I not only have experienced personally, but also am guilty of doing.

Acts 22 reminds me of God's extravagant grace toward us and how stingy we can sometimes be with His grace to others. In this chapter, Paul was rescued by the Romans from a violent mob of Jews. But Paul still held out hope for the mob. Speaking in Aramaic (a gesture of intimacy), he graciously attempted one last time to present God's message of grace by sharing his testimony.

Upon his declaration that the gospel would now be going to the gentiles, the Jewish mob was filled with rage. How dare Paul insinuate that God would extend His grace to the gentiles! Paul's encounter with the Jews in Jerusalem revealed just how far removed from God they had become.

Like so many accounts in the Old Testament, once again Israel had turned away and ceased to be grateful for God's grace and the privileges He bestowed on them. They disregarded God's voice, and became self-righteous and legalistic; they were unable to even receive, much less extend, His extravagant grace to others, because it did not fit their religious mold.

In contrast, many gentiles extended courtesy and kindness to Paul, and the gospel intrigued them. In hindsight we know that God used the Jews' rejection to fulfill His plan to take the gospel to the ends of the earth. If the Jews had embraced the gospel message, how willing would they have been to share it? Even the apostles and early church struggled and dragged their feet; the radical concept of going to the gentiles did not fit their mold.

Acts 22 presents us with a valuable lesson about not being stingy or taking God's grace for granted. Ceasing to be grateful for God's grace produces self-righteousness and legalism; disregarding His voice cultivates spiritual deafness, making us vulnerable to deception; and demanding conformity to our mold reaps an oppressed harvest. Acts 22 shows what happens when God's grace is rejected, but it also unveils His grace-filled heart toward all men.

God is constantly at work, molding us into His image. He will strategically orchestrate opportunities, stretching us to extend His grace to situations and people who do not fit our mold. When your moment comes, what kind of grace will you extend? Let us not be stingy—rather, let us be people of extravagant grace.

*–Dawn Houk, a Foursquare Navy chaplain's wife and simple church leader in Woodbridge, Va.*

### Discussion Points:

1. How easy or difficult is it for you to extend grace to others?

2. In what ways can you translate Acts 22 into a ministry plan for your church today?

3. Describe a time when someone extended extravagant grace to you.

### Prayer Points

➤ Convict me, Lord, of ways in which I try to withhold Your grace from others.

➤ Mold me into Your image, Lord.

➤ Orchestrate opportunities for me to share Your grace with anyone, just as You would.

# ACTS 22: BOLDLY SHARING YOUR TESTIMONY

BY JOHN FEHLEN

I've gone to hundreds of camps and retreats. Ever since I was young, I've been a camper, counselor, staff member, camp director or regional overseer. I've slept in too many uncomfortable bunk beds, sung lots of friendship songs and thrown plenty of pinecones into the bonfire while swaying to the melody of "It Only Takes a Spark."

Around those bonfires we would often have "testimony time." Anyone could share what God had done or was doing in his or her life. Many times the testimonies would begin with something like this: "I really didn't want to come to camp this year, but I'm so glad I did, because the Lord did some cool things in me." Other testimonies were far more dramatic. They involved crazy things that I thought happened only in R-rated movies—things like drugs or hurting people. Girls would testify to promiscuity and deep insecurity. Guys would tell us how they used to "drink, chew and date girls that do."

I recall the various testimonies I've heard at those camps and now the ones that I have the privilege of hearing as a pastor of a church, and there is an irrational thought that pops into my head almost every time: "I wish I had a testimony like that."

Now to be fair, I am grateful that I, by the grace of God, was able to side-step many tragic and life-altering pitfalls. I'm not actually wishing I had done the things I've heard others speak of—nor would I want anyone to go through such trauma—but a small part of me wonders what my testimony would sound like if it had more, well, spice.

In Acts 22, the Apostle Paul is defending himself in front of a Roman tribune. I found it interesting to note that his defense was his testimony, pure and simple. Paul addressed them with the only thing that was completely his—his testimony. No one else could claim that. No one could borrow or buy it.

Near the end of chapter 22, while the tribune was up in arms over Paul's claims, one of the centurions overheard Paul say that he was a Roman citizen. This was a deal-breaker to the case they were building against Paul. The tribune asked, "Are you a Roman citizen?" Paul said,

"Yes." They told Paul that they had gotten their citizenship by paying a large sum of money. In other words, their identity was purchased, whereas Paul was Roman by birth. When they discovered this, the tribune withdrew immediately.

Your testimony is your testimony. You can't get rid of it. There is great power in that. Nor can you borrow or purchase someone else's testimony. It's not worth it. Like me, you may have thought, "Man, I wish I could tell a shocking before-and-after story like the ones I hear others share," but honestly, it wouldn't be your story. Your story is your story; and your story, regardless of its level of "spice," is powerful.

Tell it. Speak it out. This is what we find Paul doing in chapter 22. Today I was encouraged by his boldness. I encourage you to be bold as well.

*–John Fehlen, pastor of West Salem Foursquare Church in Oregon.*

**Discussion Points:**

1. Have you ever wished for a more dramatic testimony than the one God gave you? Why or why not?

2. At what point in your life did you realize the power of your testimony, even if it wasn't so spicy?

3. What will it take for you to boldly share your story— your testimony—just like Paul did in Acts 22?

**Prayer Points:**

▸ Thank You, Lord, for the work You have done in me and for the testimony that is distinctly mine.

▸ Prepare me that I will be able to share with others what You have done for me.

▸ Convict and forgive me for times when I may shy away from sharing my testimony, and stir me to speak up whenever You want me to.

# ACTS 22: KNOWING GOD'S WORD; SPEAKING GOD'S MIND

BY LOUIE D. LOCKE

What would you say, what testimony would you share, what message would you bring if your life was on the line?

Paul's was.

The trouble and opposition that had followed Paul from place to place on his missionary journeys came to a head upon his arrival in Jerusalem. It was assumed, wrongly, that Paul had taken a gentile into the temple. Chaos ensued. Paul was attacked and beaten, and the crowds tried to tear him to pieces. Fortunately, Roman soldiers stepped in and saved his life, for the time being, and gave him an opportunity to speak.

And speak he did:

- To a hostile crowd that wanted to kill him, and saw this as a prime opportunity to do so.

- To a Roman tribunal that trying to figure out who Paul the rabble-rouser was.

- To the Sanhedrin (Jewish religious council), which was looking to build a legal case against him so he could be put to death.

How did he do it? Paul was living in the grace of the promise that Christ gave His disciples: "And when they bring you before the synagogues and the rulers and the authorities, do not be anxious about how you should defend yourself or what you should say, for the Holy Spirit will teach you in that very hour what you ought to say," (Luke 12:11-12, NKJV).

The Holy Spirit will teach you what to say.

Christ's promise.

You've filled your heart and mind with God's Word. You've looked to put into practice and obey the Lord in every area of life. If and when you're put on the spot—even hot, hot spots—don't worry. Because the Holy Spirit was given to indwell us for just such moments, and fills not only our mouth with words, but our heart with courage and boldness.

So, don't worry. Don't be anxious. Instead, give thanks that what we say at that moment of crisis (or in the grocery line) is something that will be given to us at the appropriate time by the One who will never leave, forsake or abandon us.

*—Louie D. Locke, senior pastor of Fountainhead Foursquare Church in Carson City, Nev.*

### Discussion Points:

1. Describe a time when you experienced the Holy Spirit "teaching" you exactly what you should say?

2. What does it mean to you when you read that the Holy Spirit fills not only our mouths with words, but our hearts with courage and boldness?

3. How will you know that the time is right to boldly speak the mind of God into a situation?

### Prayer Points:

▸ As I fill my mind and heart with Your Word, Lord, equip me with confidence that You are leading me.

▸ Fill my mouth with Your words, Holy Spirit, in good times and in bad.

▸ Help me speak Your mind with clarity and boldness, but not with arrogance.

# ACTS 23

*"I SHUDDER TO THINK OF THE TIMES
AS A BELIEVER THAT I HAVE ATTACKED
MY FELLOW BELIEVERS USING MY WORDS
OF SUSPICION, MISREPRESENTATION, GOSSIP
AND ANGER. I'M GRATEFUL FOR THE
FORGIVENESS I HAVE RECEIVED FROM
THOSE I HAVE HURT, INCLUDING JESUS,
WHO FELT THE STING AS WELL."*
**—JIM SCOTT**

# ACTS 22-23: WE ARE NOT ALONE

BY JIM SCOTT

"Now it happened, as I journeyed and came near Damascus at about noon, suddenly a great light from heaven shone around me. And I fell to the ground and heard a voice saying to me, 'Saul, Saul, why are you persecuting Me?' So I answered, 'Who are You, Lord?' And He said to me, 'I am Jesus of Nazareth, whom you are persecuting'" (Acts 22:6-8, NKJV).

As far as we know from the Scriptures, the apostle Paul (as the Pharisee Saul) never met Jesus during His ministry in Israel. And while this is something of an argument from silence, there were many times in the Acts narrative and in Paul's teachings, debates and the defense of his apostolic ministry when the sharing of this significant experience in his journey would have added weight or a counterpoint to what he was writing or saying.

If it is true that Saul (soon to become Paul) had never met Jesus in life and, as a result, would not have been one of the leaders who sought to destroy Him, nor one who sat in judgment over Him, what could Jesus have meant when He confronted him with these words, "I am Jesus of Nazareth, whom you are persecuting."

Saul, in his persecutions, terror and murder, had no idea that there was another who was also experiencing the horror of his evil work, Jesus the Nazarene.

In this moment, Saul's discovery confirms for all time that Jesus is keeping His promises to His people, the sheep of His pasture: "For where two or three are gathered together in My name, I am there in the midst of them," (Matt. 18:20, NKJV); "I will never leave you nor forsake you" (Heb. 13:5); and "I am with you always, even to the end of the age" (Matt. 28:20).

Indeed, our Jesus is Immanuel, God with us (see Matt. 1:23)!

Jesus was with the first believers as they were persecuted and harmed, and He so closely identified with them that He said to Saul: "Why are you persecuting me? ... I am Jesus the Nazarene, the one you are persecuting." To attack one of Jesus' disciples is to attack Jesus Himself!

I shudder to think of the times as a believer that I have attacked my fellow believers using my words of suspicion, misrepresentation, gossip and anger. I'm grateful for the forgiveness I have received from those I have hurt, including Jesus, who felt the sting as well.

I'm also strengthened and encouraged. I think of all those times I knew I could get through a painful season if only Jesus were with me, and He was! Each time I would cry out to Jesus, hoping that He knew my heartache, fear and loss, and He did.

Amazingly, incredibly, Jesus is with us, suffering with us. Then, as the King of His kingdom, He helps us as One closer than a brother with all we need. With great power He heals, delivers and restores us for His glory!

*–Jim Scott, Foursquare vice president of global operations, director of Foursquare Missions International.*

### Discussion Points:

1. Discuss the significance of this statement: "Amazingly, incredibly, Jesus is with us, suffering with us."

2. Describe an encounter you had with the Holy Spirit where He pointed out your weakness of accusation, suspicion, anger or criticism toward others.

3. Talk about the forgiveness that came as you repented for those failings.

### Prayer Points:

- Thank you, Lord, for going through every life circumstance with me.

- Forgive me for any indifference I may have had about the suffering of others.

- Show me anyone whom I should apologize to for my insensitivity to their needs.

# ACTS 23: STEWARDING HEALTHY RELATIONSHIPS

BY GLENN BURRIS JR.

Reading about the dispute that broke out between the Pharisees and the Sadducees in Acts 23 reminds me of some fierce rivalries that have existed around the world, many of which still exist today.

Sometimes it seems easier to remember what people disagree about than what they agree on. History often remembers more about what divided people than what unified them. Hollywood's most popular films often center on some sort of conflict that makes the script riveting to its viewers.

Since the fall of man, we've found ourselves in a broken world that desperately needs healing. From the incredible rage of Cain in Genesis 4 to the present rise of revolts around the world, we find ourselves constantly at war, sometimes even from within.

Conflict is healthy sometimes, but a constant grinding that disrupts our commitment to the good of others is destructive. When we only see life from our perspective, it limits our ability to relate to others.

The writer of Hebrews says, "For we do not have a High Priest who cannot sympathize with our weaknesses" (Hebrews 4:15a, NKJV). Jesus chose to experience life from our perspective.

When you find yourself in a serious point of conflict, stop speaking, and listen. Hear them out. Don't begin by feeling threatened. Start by being open. Perhaps the Lord will use that opportunity for you to gain a better understanding of the "reason" behind their intensity or their pain.

It's more important to build a bridge than it is to make sure that your point is heard. I'm sure that some of the Hatfields and the McCoys didn't even know why there was a feud raging between their families. But they sure seemed convinced that there was a good reason why they were bitter enemies, even though they couldn't tell you what that reason was.

The clear division of the religious sects within the Jewish community in Paul's day bore no positive witness to the God they claimed to serve. Their value was defined by their ability to staunchly defend their positions. Although throughout history the Lord had demonstrated His commitment to forgive, repair, love and reconcile, they were content only when others capitulated to their perspective.

How sad it is when we steward our words and actions to tearing down others instead of building them up.

The one indisputable witness to the world is our love toward one another! Don't waste another minute stewarding a broken or significantly strained relationship. God took the first step toward you. Perhaps you should take the first step toward someone else—today!

*–Glenn Burris Jr., president of The Foursquare Church.*

**Discussion Points:**

1. How have you learned to see life from the perspective of others?

2. How do you share those skills with people you teach and disciple?

3. Is there someone you will take a step toward in order to heal a broken relationship?

**Prayer Points**

- Overflow me with Your love and grace so that my life is characterized by healthy relationships.

- Keep me focused on health with others rather than on broken or strained relationships.

- Motivate me, Lord, to take the first step toward someone with love today.

# ACTS 23: RECOGNIZING GOD'S PLAN

BY TIM CLARK

"But the following night the Lord stood by him and said, 'Be of good cheer, Paul; for as you have testified for Me in Jerusalem, vwso you must also bear witness at Rome'" (Acts 23:11, NKJV).

Paul found himself mired in a massive storm that was threatening to take him out. He had been rejected by the Jewish leaders. His ministry plans had been shut down. He was a Roman prisoner. People were actively plotting against his life.

In the middle of all this, Jesus stood near Paul.

Do you understand that whatever you may be facing, Jesus is standing near you? When you are thrown a huge curveball in life, Jesus is not far away.

And He tells you the same thing He told Paul that night: "Take courage; I have an assignment for you."

You may be bankrupt, emotionally stretched, and physically on the ropes, but as long as you are still alive, there is a purpose for your existence. You may feel like you are in prison and that others want to see your life finished, but God is bigger than all of that.

In the fifth chapter of Philippians, Paul wrote that he had learned the secret to being content whatever the circumstance. He also wrote in Phil. 4:6-7, "Be anxious for nothing, but in everything by prayer and supplication, with thanksgiving, let your requests be made known to God; and the peace of God, which surpasses all understanding, will guard your hearts and minds through Christ Jesus." And all this was written from a prison cell to some folks who had met him after being beaten and thrown into yet another prison.

"Take courage; I still have an important assignment for you." Listen to Jesus right now. He is with you and has a plan for your life—and it is a plan for you to make a difference in the world. As long as

He is your Lord and as long as you are alive, He has a mission in which you are called to participate. And in fact, the reality of your situation may be that He is using it to put you right where He wants you to be for His glory.

Don't let any circumstance or challenge cause you to imagine He is not right there with you, or that He isn't actively involved in working out His plan in and through you.

*–Tim Clark, district supervisor of the Greater Los Angeles District.*

### Discussion Points:

1. Reflect on a time when you were thrown a huge curveball in life but knew that Jesus was standing near you. What did you know, sense and believe about that situation?

2. What does Phil. 5 look like in your life as God shows you His plan?

3. How can you successfully resist the enemy's attempt to dissuade you from God's plan for your life?

### Prayer Points:

▶ You are aware of what I am facing today, Lord, and I trust You to help get me through.

▶ Fill me with courage that I will be able to see Your plan at work in every part of my life.

▶ I'm listening right now, Lord; speak Your Word to me and show me Your plan.

# ACTS 24

*"HAVING A CLEAR CONSCIENCE BEFORE
GOD AND MAN IS MORE THAN JUST THE
ABILITY TO LOOK YOURSELF IN THE MIRROR;
IT IS SEEING HIM FACE TO FACE!"*
—*LARRY SPOUSTA*

# ACTS 24: FOR THE SAKE OF A CLEAR CONSCIENCE

BY LARRY SPOUSTA

Approaching each new day with a clear conscience is perhaps one of the best feelings in the world. I remember a few right choices from youth made in response to my father's oft-repeated question, "Will you be able to look yourself in the mirror come morning?" Ah, yes, haunting words that still keep me on the straight and narrow!

A conscience free from compromise—a life lived with biblical convictions—remains the distinguishing mark of a heart yielded to Christ.

The apostle Paul, though not perfect in every response (e.g., his reference to the high priest as a "whitewashed wall" comes to mind), exemplifies a man who had surrendered his life fully to the Son of God.

In complete obedience he made an ill-advised trip to Jerusalem and found himself the target of angry Jewish assassins. Rescued by soldiers and whisked away to Caesarea, Paul was allowed to appear before Governor Felix.

The charges were serious. The accusations of Jewish leaders were padded with exaggeration and described Paul as a plague, a creator of dissension and a ringleader of a seditious sect who had defiled the Temple. The use of such superlatives suggests that the apostle to the gentiles must have upset the standard operating procedures of the Jewish religious system.

Contrary to his accusers, Paul's defense cut past the verbal embellishments to the heart of the confrontation. "I have hope in God, which they themselves also accept, that there will be a resurrection of the dead, both of the just and the unjust. This being so, I myself always strive to have a conscience without offense toward God and men" (Acts 24:15-16, NKJV).

Paul was not an insurrectionist; he was a believer in the resurrection! As such, faith kept his actions and speech centered in Christ's power and his conscience safely harbored in the truth.

Leaders of every variety—pastors, supervisors, missionaries and denominational executives—face circumstances that threaten to muddy a clear conscience. False accusations tempt us to speak harshly. Exaggeration of the facts can and will sidetrack us from the bedrock cause of a dispute. Honest communication is lost to the fear of personal or professional repercussion.

Paul had a lot to lose. His life and his freedom were at stake. Even so, he fearlessly and with firm conviction spoke of the glorious hope of the resurrection. In essence, he was confessing, "One day I will stand before God and give account for my life and behavior; I don't want to be ashamed."

Having a clear conscience before God and man is more than just the ability to look yourself in the mirror; it is seeing Him face to face!

–Larry Spousta, supervisor of the North Pacific District.


**Discussion Points:**

1. How do you think a person can live with a clear conscience before God and man?

2. Describe how you are able to live life this way.

3. Explain the significance of this statement: "Having a clear conscience before God and man is more than just the ability to look yourself in the mirror; it is seeing Him face to face!"

**Prayer Points**

➤ Holy Spirit, transform my thinking and my behavior so that I honor You in everything I do.

➤ Teach me to live and lead consistent with Your Word and without regret.

➤ Confirm Your presence in my life, and let me be a genuine reflection of You to others.

# ACTS 24: THE ACT OF MY REACTIONS

BY DAN MUNDT

Reading through the book of Acts these last two years, I have been amazed and challenged to learn from what I've read and to live it each day.

In the beginning, as I read one chapter each day, I was most excited about setting up my heart and ministry for miracles of multiplication. I have since learned that Acts is also about how we live daily in a culture that is not church-friendly. It's about how we act in a way that shows the power of Christ's love.

In Acts 24, Paul's life-journey gives us an example of responding to those who reject Jesus and "spitefully use you" (Matt. 5:44, NKJV). Paul was falsely accused by religious leaders, and then protected from an ambush and taken by a security army to Caesarea to appear before Governor Felix. Through it all, we see Paul's response guided by the power of the Holy Spirit and the evidence of his deep relationship with Jesus.

In the middle of much pressure, Paul did not lose his joy. He answered the governor by saying, "I do the more cheerfully answer for myself," (Acts 24:10, NKJV).

When I read this, I asked myself how I would react under such pressure.

Whatever you and I face today, joy is the deep abiding work of the Holy Spirit in us, and my prayer is that we don't lose our joy during seasons of stress.

Paul did not forget his message, even under extreme circumstances. Paul spoke his message clearly: "I have hope in God, which they themselves also accept, that there will be a resurrection of the dead, both of the just and the unjust. This being so, I myself always strive to have a conscience without offense toward God and men" (vv. 15-16).

In our world today, the enemy has worked hard to diminish our voice and confuse our message. In response, may we raise our voices with a clear message that Jesus is our only hope for resurrection to eternal life.

We also learn a lesson from Paul that he did not lose sight of his purpose. In the middle of persecution, slander, injustice and imprisonment, the purposes of God were fulfilled in Paul's life and ministry as he shared the gospel with Felix and his wife.

Oh, by the way, Paul also had to be patient as he was held for more than two years. At the end of the day, Felix—the very person Paul had preached Christ to—left office and left Paul bound in chains.

May the Lord be glorified in our lives today as we serve with joy and preach the message of His love and forgiveness, all while being patient, not losing sight of His purpose in and through us every day.
*–Dan Mundt, district supervisor, Heartland District.*

**Discussion Points:**

1. The enemy has worked hard to diminish our voice and confuse our message. In response, how will you raise your voice with a clear message that Jesus is our only hope for resurrection to eternal life?

2. In difficult times, do you act and react with godly joy? Why or why not?

3. How do you stay focused on God's purpose for your life even when challenges come your way?

**Prayer Points:**

- Jesus, You are our only hope for the resurrection and eternal life; Help me always thank you!

- When I forget the eternal nature of our faith, O God, please jolt my memory.

- Let my reactions be those that demonstrate full alignment with Your desire, Lord.

# ACTS 24: MAKING THE MOST OF OPPORTUNITIES

BY LOUIE D. LOCKE

Two years.

That's the amount of time Paul waited in a Caesarean jail cell for his legal case to be acted upon by the governor.

Those two years pass in one sentence: "But after two years Porcius Festus succeeded Felix; and Felix, wanting to do the Jews a favor, left Paul bound" (Acts 24:27, NKJV).

Two years.

In that time, Paul's testifying about his court case and the charges against him morphed into regular opportunities to give witness to his faith through conversations with the governor. Further, he shared with all who would listen about "righteousness, self-control and the judgment to come" (v. 25).

And instead of getting bitter, wondering how God could forget him in Caesarea—after all, didn't Paul have God's promise that he would testify in Rome?—Paul used the challenging circumstances of prison to encourage others through letters that we now refer to as Ephesians, Philippians and Colossians, to name a few.

Two years.

Paul saw it not as a waste of his time, but as an opportunity from the Lord.

"But I want you to know, brethren, that the things which happened to me have actually turned out for the furtherance of the gospel, so that it has become evident to the whole palace guard, and to all the rest, that my chains are in Christ; and most of the brethren in the

Lord, having become confident by my chains, are much more bold to speak the word without fear" (Phil. 1:12-14).

Two years.

Lord, I pray you give us eyes to see our lives and circumstances, come what may, as God-given opportunities. And may Paul's words from his jail cell ring in our ears: "Rejoice in the Lord always; again I will say, rejoice!" (Phil. 4:4).

*–Louie Locke, senior pastor of Fountainhead Foursquare Church in Carson City, Nev.*

**Discussion Points:**

1. How long have you had to wait for God's promise to be fulfilled? What was your reaction to waiting—to God, and to other people?

2. Describe any ministry opportunities that emerged during the time you had to wait for God's promise to be fulfilled.

3. How difficult is it to "rejoice in the Lord always" while you are waiting for God to come through?

**Prayer Points:**

- I recognize that no matter how long it takes, if I learn what You are teaching me, the time is never wasted.

- Circumstances may seem daunting, but as long as You are with me, they will not overwhelm me.

- In the best of times and the worst of times, Lord, I will exalt Your Name, for You are holy.

# ACTS 25

*"PAUL WAS WILLING TO BE ACCOUNTABLE FOR HIS ACTIONS AND WAS COMPLETELY CONFIDENT THAT THE LORD WOULD BE HIS DEFENDER."*
*—RON THIGPENN*

# ACTS 25: PAYING THE PRICE FOR GODLY CONFIDENCE

BY RON THIGPENN

As I read Acts 25, the thing that stands out to me is how Paul remained steadfast in his profession of faith and commitment to the Lord Jesus, even after having been unjustly held in prison for two years without being brought to trial.

When he was finally brought before Festus, Paul said: "For if I am an offender, or have committed anything deserving of death, I do not object to dying; but if there is nothing in these things of which these men accuse me, no one can deliver me to them" (Acts 25:11, NJKV).

Paul was willing to be accountable for his actions and was completely confident that the Lord would be his defender.

There are three important points I believe the Lord wants us to catch here:

- **Our walk must be consistent with our profession of faith.**
  We must live what we say we believe. That doesn't mean we are expected to be perfect, but it does mean that we must have hearts submitted to the will of God and be attuned to the Spirit of God so that when we do get off track, we hear the correction of the Holy Spirit, repent and immediately make the necessary changes to get back on track.

- **We must be accountable for our actions.**
  Even after we repent for wrong actions, we are still accountable for the consequences of those actions. Paul was fully ready to pay the price—even to be put to death—for anything he had done wrong. Living with that kind of accountability will help us to be more careful in the things we say and do.

- **We must have full confidence in the Lord's ability and willingness to deliver us.**

Paul had complete confidence that the Lord would deliver him. He did not try to manipulate the situation. During the two years Paul was in prison, the previous governor, Felix, would periodically bring Paul out, hoping that Paul would offer him a bribe to be released. All Paul did was continue to share his faith in Christ with him. I have heard multiple voices within the church recently preaching the message that God is calling us to return to our first love; to love Jesus and serve Him in total submission and humility; and to return to the simplicity of the truth of the gospel.

I believe God is calling us to live with the same confidence and boldness that Paul did. To live lives sold out to Jesus at every level. To be confident in Whom we serve, knowing that He is faithful to deliver us in every situation when we walk in obedience.

*–Ron Thigpenn, vice president and chief financial officer for The Foursquare Church.*

### Discussion Points:

1. How do you ensure that your walk is consistent with your talk?

2. Describe a time when you were required to pay the price for wrongdoing, even though the Lord forgave you.

3. We, like Paul, are called to repent and walk worthy of our calling; just how do you intend to do that?

### Prayer Points

▶ Fill me, Holy Spirit, so I can live out what I say I believe.

▶ I will remember that You are my first love and live my life with You at the center.

▶ Help me live in boldness and confidence based solely on Your promise and provision.

# ACTS 25: BECOMING RESISTANT TO NONSENSE

BY TIM CLARK

"For if I am an offender or have committed anything deserving of death, I do not object to dying; but if there is nothing in these things of which these men accuse me, no one can deliver me to them. I appeal to Caesar" (Acts 25:11, NKJV).

Some Christians seem to have a confidence problem: They get internally discouraged when they face opposition, but externally they don't feel it is right to push back.

I understand the call to humility; Jesus not only told us to turn the other cheek, but He also modeled this when He was on trial for His life. When being accused, Jesus didn't say a word—and that led to His unjust execution.

Paul clearly didn't take that route. Repeatedly he seemed to say, "I'm not going to let anybody push me around," and he fully used the legal system to ensure that his old peers, the twisted religious leaders, didn't have a leg to stand on when they tried to go after him. I love The Message translation: "Nobody can force me to go along with their nonsense" (Acts 25:11).

So the question is, when is it OK to push back, and when is it proper to stay silent and nonresistant?

I'm not so sure there is an easy answer, but I do have some thoughts:

1.  If you are externally compliant but internally seething at your treatment, and you are bitter and unforgiving toward those who are hostile to you, not being vocally honest is only going to hurt you. Passive-aggressive attitudes or actions are never kingdom-compliant.

2.  If you have done something to deserve the treatment you are getting, step up and own it. Paul says, "If I've done something deserving death, then

punish me properly." Most of us have not done anything deserving death, but if we have made mistakes and are facing opposition because of those mistakes, we shouldn't over-spiritualize it and claim persecution by the enemy. Admit your failure, take your lumps and move on (hopefully having learned something in the process).

3. If someone is accusing you wrongfully, don't just lay down and let them roll over you. There are appropriate times to defend ourselves, not because we are worried about us, but as agents of the kingdom there is a "violent" aspect to pressing in with the Good News. The enemy will use people to try to silence the truth or stop God's progress through us; we owe it to our assignment to stand up for truth when a lie is being told.

4. Finally, there are some times—and we need to be spiritually sensitive to them—when we have done nothing, but the proper response to the persecution is not to push back, but to be silent. We may be called to this when the result of the opposition will actually further God's purposes. Even though the accusation against Him was completely erroneous, Jesus endured the cross. As agents of His kingdom, there will be times when we are also called to "…consider Him who endured such hostility from sinners against Himself" (Heb. 12:3, NKJV) and likewise receive unjust hostility for the larger purposes of God.

*–Tim Clark, district supervisor of the Greater Los Angeles District.*

### Discussion Points:

1. When do you think it is okay to push back, and when is it proper to stay silent and non-resistant?

2. Have you ever encountered a person whom the enemy tried to use to silence God's progress? How was the situation resolved?

3. Explain why you either agree or disagree with this statement: "There will be times when we are called to 'consider Him who endured from sinners such hostility against himself' and likewise receive unjust hostility for the larger purposes of God."

### Prayer Points:

▸ Challenge any tendency in me to become passive-aggressive, Lord, even if I feel justified.

▸ Soften my heart so I will repent of any wrongdoing.

▸ Teach me to discern when I should stand up for myself and when I should remain silent.

# ACTS 25: FINDING OUR SOURCE OF CONFIDENCE

BY JOHN FEHLEN

There is a big difference between confidence and cockiness. Acts 25 portrays Paul as confident.

There is also a big difference between being blameless and sinless. Acts 25 portrays Paul also as blameless.

Imagine being blameless—I mean, really, totally blameless.

Most of us would be hard pressed to claim that title. Frankly it's not a title we should bestow upon ourselves anyway. It's much better coming from others.

The Bible tells us in Genesis 6:9 that Noah was blameless.

In Job 1:1 we read, "There was a man in the land of Uz, whose name was Job; and that man was blameless and upright, and one who feared God and shunned evil" (NKJV).

Neither of these men was sinless, because that is a description reserved for Jesus only. But they were denoted as blameless. Such is the case with the Apostle Paul. Throughout Acts 25, the ruling leaders simply couldn't prove any charges of wrongdoing for which he was being held (v. 7). Paul's accusers struggled to pin anything on him. Everyone was at a loss as to how to investigate the charges brought against him.

Paul was blameless.

He was also confident. I shudder when I read verse 11: "For if I am an offender, or have committed anything deserving of death, I do not object to dying; but if there is nothing in these things of which these men accuse me, no one can deliver me to them. I appeal to Caesar."

*Whoa,* Caesar. Paul pulled out the big guns. Now, that's confidence.

The reason Paul could appeal to Caesar is because he knew he was not at fault. The most durable confidence is that which is built upon blamelessness. Did you catch that? Confidence flows from blamelessness.

*–John Fehlen, pastor of West Salem Foursquare Church in Oregon.*

### Discussion Points:

1. Describe your understanding of the difference between "blameless" and "sinless."

2. What similarities are there between your situation today and Paul's appeal to Caesar in Acts 25?

3. In what ways will you draw personal confidence from your blameless standing in Christ?

**Prayer Points:**

▸ Cleanse me, God, so that I may stand blameless in Christ.

▸ As I stand blameless in Christ, increase my confidence in all You are doing in my life.

▸ With boldness, allow Your life to flow confidently from me to everyone I meet.

# ACTS 26

*"PAUL UNDERLINED THAT HIS MESSAGE WASN'T JUST ABOUT REPENTANCE. HE ALSO PREACHED ABOUT A LIFESTYLE THAT PROVES A CHANGE HAS TAKEN PLACE ON THE INSIDE."*
**—DAVID WHEELER**

# ACTS 24-26: BEING A PERSON WHO MAKES THE DIFFERENCE

BY GLENN BURRIS JR.

Acts 24-26 includes quite a list of influential leaders from the day. And, they all were involved in deciding the fate of the Apostle Paul.

There is Ananias, the high priest; Tertullus, the lawyer; Felix, the governor; Felix's replacement, Festus; and finally, King Agrippa. You could recite their pedigrees of experience and education, but not one of them seemed to be able to step back, ask the right questions and get a sense of the bigger picture as it related to what was happening in their midst.

The decisions these leaders made seemed to be based more on appeasing the crowd or technically following the law, not on discerning the right decision.

Have we become too busy to step back and ask the important questions? Do we think we already know the answers? Do we have an opinion about the issue that keeps us from being swayed differently? Are we afraid to speak up? Has it become too easy to go with the flow?

Recently, I realized I missed the chance to make a difference. Afterward, I had a long plane ride to think about my decision!

Waiting in line outside the baggage drop at John F. Kennedy International Airport in New York, I was frustrated while watching a scene unfold for nearly 25 minutes. A single man and a couple appeared to be traveling together, and they were trying to get their bags checked for an international flight.

Apparently there was a language barrier, but in the end the conflict seemed to be about money, baggage fees and airline policies. They needed to pay extra money for their bags but only had cash. The airline employee would only accept a credit card for payment.

These folks had passports, boarding passes and cash, but no credit cards. It was rainy, cold and frustrating.

There was a moment—and I remember it vividly—when I could have stepped in, used my credit card, paid for their bags and helped them on their way. It also would have freed up the growing line of frustrated flyers, and prevented the three from having to reload their bags and navigate their way through the crowded terminal.

I'm pretty sure they weren't frequent fliers, so this turn of events was going to extend their busy morning.

My failure was not that I was truly obligated, but rather that I wasn't responsive to the Holy Spirit. I don't think I'm supposed to pay every time I see someone struggling like these folks were, but I distinctly remember the moment where I was being prodded to step in … and I didn't.

I found out that you have a lot of time to think about "what if?" while on a six-hour, cross-country flight.

I'm only trying to communicate that everyday situations come across our paths that are God-arranged. I took a few simple lessons away from what I experienced that day:

- When you are responsive to the Lord, others are helped, and you are left with a sense of fulfillment.

- When life has become so matter-of-fact that you miss Him, repent; start listening and looking again.

- When you get cynical or calloused toward a situation or others, remember that you have been a recipient of His help on more than one occasion, even when you didn't deserve it.

- Your intervention just may spark a rise of hope and faith in the recipient.

Finally, an impressive resumé of education and experience may have mattered to those leaders in that list in Acts 24-26. But in the end, what matters most is whether you are listening and learning before you lead.

Some situations are looking for just one person to make the difference. Be that person.

*–Glenn Burris Jr., president of The Foursquare Church.*

### Discussion Points:

1. Describe a situation in which you were able to make the difference for another person.

2. How does that memory influence your ability to help someone else?

3. When cynicism creeps in, how will you resensitize your mind and your spirit to recognize an opportunity to make a difference?

### Prayer Points:

▸ Life gets pretty hectic, Lord, but help me slow down enough to see ways that I can help others.

▸ I remember how You have delivered me; help me grant that same grace to someone else today.

▸ Strengthen me to be a person who makes the difference.

# ACTS 26: PRODUCING SPIRITUAL FRUIT IN EVERY CIRCUMSTANCE

BY DAVID WHEELER

Acts 26 is chock full of material for a devotion.

Here we have Paul, the eloquent evangelist, "sharing his story" (for you postmoderns) or "giving his testimony" (for the rest of you), in an apparent attempt to win King Agrippa to the Christian cause.

Of course, there is the retelling of Paul's encounter with Christ, where we catch a glimpse of God's plan to rescue gentiles and give them a place among His people.

This truly is a remarkable event in history, and we are benefactors of this gracious gift. Paul underlined that his message wasn't just about repentance. He also preached about a lifestyle that proves a change has taken place on the inside.

But I don't want to talk about any of these things. Instead, I want to talk about the last verse of Acts 26. It may seem insignificant to some, but it has bugged me for a long time. It tells us that Paul could have been set free if he had not appealed to Caesar.

During a recent devotional with the Foursquare Missions International (FMI) staff, I brought up the fact that I struggle with this verse and what it implies. I inquired: "Did Paul jump the gun by appealing to Caesar? Did he not trust the Lord to deliver him earlier, and consequently had to pay with his freedom?"

FMI Director Jim Scott then brought up a really good point. He asked how much of this outlook is framed around a Western ideal that freedom is somehow linked with the absence of hardship, struggle and pain.

Fortunately for us, Paul responded differently than we sometimes do today. He wrote his letters to the Colossians, Ephesians, Philippians, and to his friend Philemon while incarcerated in Rome.

In reality, the reason I have struggled with this passage is that I see myself in it. In difficult times I have often wondered: "Lord, did I do something wrong to get into this tough spot? Could I have avoided this pain, hurt or struggle?"

Perhaps it would be better to ask: "God, what are You doing right now? How may I be a part of it?" Like Paul, may we all come to the place where we can produce great fruit for the kingdom of God, no matter in what circumstance we find ourselves.

*–David Wheeler, Foursquare Missions International Go Teams coordinator.*

### Discussion Points:

1. When you encounter challenges, do you immediately look for a way out? Or do you grow right where you are?

2. What is your expectation about producing spiritual fruit? Do you require perfect conditions or will you be available to produce this fruit in every circumstance?

3. What are the benefits of asking, "God, what are You doing right now? How may I be a part of it?"

### Prayer Points

➤ Please show me Your purposes for my circumstances, Lord, especially when I don't understand them.

➤ Direct my response to circumstances so that the kingdom of God will be stronger in the end.

➤ Change my attitude about what I consider "difficult," and let me be willing to do whatever You think is necessary to spread the gospel.

# ACTS 26: OBEDIENCE TO GOD'S VISION

BY TIM CLARK

"…I was not disobedient to the heavenly vision" (Acts 26:19, NKJV).

I've heard it said that good ideas are easier to find than sand on a beach. If you talk to a visionary, a leader or a dreamer, it's likely that you won't be able to keep track of all the wonderful plans or thoughts going on inside his or her head. There is no shortage of people who feel they have heard things from God that, if put into practice, would change the world.

So why isn't the world getting changed? If ideas are everywhere, so are people who don't execute those ideas. Paul wasn't going to be one of those people who wouldn't follow through; he called it being obedient to the vision from heaven. He received a picture and then spent the rest of his life passionately pursuing the completion of that target.

In business and the arts, this follow-through is often what separates those who dream about getting things done and those who actually do it. In the kingdom, it is what separates those who are obedient or disobedient to God's voice.

Do you have a vision—a God-given picture of something that will change your world? Start putting your energy into seeing it happen. Pray, plan, pursue and promote that thing. If God is in it, He will provide the resource to make it happen, but we are still called to work. Paul said in 1 Cor. 3 that God makes a seed grow, but we are responsible to plant and water and cultivate to create conditions for healthy growth to happen.

And what if you think you have a vision from God, but you find out later that you were wrong? I've always said that I would rather give my whole life to following the voice of Jesus even if I find out later that I got something wrong, than to think I'm hearing Jesus and not respond to what I understand as His voice, even if later I discover it wasn't Him. In other words, I believe God will honor attempted but misdirected obedience, but He will not work through the lives of those who think they are hearing but who don't respond to those impressions.

The Holy Spirit changed the world through Paul because he was available to follow God at every turn, and was totally sold out to everything he understood he was hearing from the Lord. I don't think it's rocket science; we obey what God says (the vision) the best we possibly can, and then God makes it grow.

*–Tim Clark, district supervisor of the Greater Los Angeles District.*

### Discussion Points:

1. Why is it the world is not being changed even though there are so many great ideas about changing the world?

2. Have you ever thought you had a vision from God but you find out later that you were wrong? What did you learn from that experience—about God and about yourself?

3. What specific steps will you take in an obedient response to what you hear God saying?

### Prayer Points:

▸ Clarify for me, Lord, what Your vision is for my life and for my ministry.

▸ Align my attitudes, thoughts, behaviors and relationships to fully embrace Your vision for me.

▸ Strengthen me to passionately pursue Your vision with excellence and obedience.

# ACTS 27

*"...WE SERVE A GOD WHO POWERFULLY SHOWS UP IN THE MIDDLE OF THE MOST DESPERATE CIRCUMSTANCES WE FACE. NOT ONLY IS GOD PRESENT, BUT ALSO HE IS A GOD WHOSE WHISPERED PROMISES CAN PENETRATE THE MOST BURDENED AND FRIGHTENED HEART WITH TRUTH..."*
**—JENNA JAVINS**

# ACTS 27: CONQUERING FEAR IN THE FACE OF ADVERSITY

BY GLENN BURRIS JR.

Paul set sail for Rome in Acts 27. The Holy Spirit and others had warned him that the conclusion of his earthly ministry, and his life, were at hand.

Still, he pressed on.

In fact, this particular storm—much like a nor'easter—raged out of control and brought experienced sailors to the brink of despair. They had already thrown the tackle and the cargo overboard. The writer of Acts concluded that everyone had lost any hope of being saved (see Acts 27:20).

Surely you've been at a place where life or ministry has worn you down. The constant pressure has stripped you of any fight; the little courage you mustered has left the room; and now, you're looking for the first door that will open.

Any door will do. And therein lies the problem—"any door." It's the place that the enemy of our souls likes to get us: a place where any option will do. Somehow at times like this, we instinctively know that such an escape might relieve the immediate pain, but it also has the potential to leave a much bigger wake.

But we're desperate.

Debbie and I faced a season like this early in our ministry. I took the first option. I announced my resignation and accepted a new ministry position that would get us "out of Dodge." The problem was that God had not opened this door. But in the heat of the moment, anything seemed better than where we were—at least, I thought so at the moment.

God spoke to me so clearly that this was not His will. He had been mostly silent until that point. I had to repent and was afforded grace and mercy to back out of a commitment that was quite public. The willingness to admit wrong and make the adjustment laid a foundation for the rest of our ministry decisions.

Courage isn't always grabbing the sword and being the first one to charge up the hill. Andy Stanley recently said three things about courage that I'd like to share with you:

1. Courage is staying when it would be easier to go (Joseph, Mary's fiancé).
2. Courage is going when it would be easier to stay (Abraham).
3. Courage is asking for help when it would be easier to go it alone (Hezekiah).

Paul got a revelation while on his way to Rome aboard that ship. He strongly proclaimed that everyone on the ship would be saved, "if they stayed with the ship" (see v. 31). The crew cut loose the lifeboats, just in case anyone didn't believe that Paul had received this revelation from the Lord. Every life was spared because they resisted their fears and obeyed the direction of the Lord.

The real enemy we all face is fear in the face of adversity. Such fear will always point us in the wrong direction. Why shouldn't it? Lucifer is the father of lies, so we should expect those seeds to be planted.

Resist giving in to your fears. Those defining moments or tipping points will determine whether your life is lived in a constant state of turmoil or whether you will reverse course and discover God's peace and will for your life.

What we really need is a revelation. "Ask, and it will be given to you; seek, and you will find; knock, and it will be opened to you" (Matt. 7:7, NKJV).

*—Glenn Burris Jr., president of The Foursquare Church.*

### Discussion Points:

1. Describe a time when you took the first door of escape from a difficult situation. What happened as a result?

2. In what ways have you been successful resisting fear in ministry?

3. Interact with this statement: "Resist giving in to your fears. Those defining moments, or tipping points, will determine whether your life is lived in a constant state of turmoil or whether you will reverse course and discover God's peace and will for your life."

### Prayer Points

▸ Keep me moving in the right direction, Lord, even when I am tempted to make a break for the nearest exit.

▸ I pray for the strength to stand firm in faith, especially when adversity strikes.

▸ Reveal Your ways to me so I have Your assurance that I'm doing the right thing.

# ACTS 27: BELIEVING DURING THE STORM

BY JENNA JAVINS

Amidst the sailing adventures of Acts 27, we catch a glimpse of the promises of God invading desperate circumstances.

Paul was a prisoner aboard a ship being pummeled by rough seas, encountering a tremendous loss of provision, and facing the ultimate threat of being shipwrecked. The captain's disregard for sound warnings led Paul and all of the passengers into grave danger.

It was in the midst of this scene that God chose to speak. His message of hope intersected desperation with a promise echoing louder than the perilous storm raging about them. God spoke a promise of safety and protection that required a response of faith; faith expressed through actions.

As the storm continued to rage fiercely about them, Paul proclaimed God's message of deliverance as he stood steady, believing his "Promiser." Paul's faith, fueled by his identity rooted in God, was proved authentic through the storm.

Though their fears were valid, Paul's fellow shipmates were confronted with the choice to join him in faith or abandon ship, hoping for survival another way. While waves crashed and winds whipped through the deck of the battered and beaten ship, Paul issued his call to faith once again, and his shipmates responded in belief in Paul's God.

In an extreme act of faith, the soldiers cut the ropes that secured their lifeboats, severing all ties to a Plan B.

Reflecting on these passages stirs my heart to remember that we serve a God who powerfully shows up in the middle of the most desperate circumstances we face. Not only is God present, but also He is a God whose whispered promises can penetrate the most burdened and frightened heart with truth; and His truth always brings a rescue.

Like the men aboard the ship that day, God offers us a choice. When His whispers echo into the storms of our circumstances, will we respond in faith and trust, or abandon ship, hoping for a Plan B?

Faith means taking God at His Word and severing all ties to Plan B. This is the kind of faith that moves the heart of God in rescue and, in the end, pleases Him.

*–Jenna Javins served with Foursquare Missions International as youth pastor at Mochudi Foursquare Church in Botswana. She currently is a youth minister and missions/outreach mentor at Westside Church in Bend, Ore.*

### Discussion Points:

1. Have you ever experienced something like this storm—a life-threatening experience that you were sure would kill you? How did your faith in Christ bring you through?

2. How does a person develop the ability to hear the voice of God during such a traumatic episode?

3. When you "cut the ropes" of a potential "Plan B," what do you need to know in order to stand and believe in God?

### Prayer Points:

- Your truth always brings deliverance; I need You to show up in power for me today.

- I commit to ride out my current storm, Lord, knowing that You are there with me.

- There is no "plan B," and I know that Your plans for me always include hope for the future.

# ACTS 27: STUCK ON GOD'S ABILITY TO HELP

BY LOUIE D. LOCKE

Paul and 275 others were in trouble. Their tiny ship was sailing toward Italy and had been caught in a winter storm that raged without stopping for more than two weeks. It was so severe that the most experienced sailors had given up all hope of surviving (Acts 27:20).

But not Paul—he knew that God had told him he would witness on His behalf before Caesar in Rome (Acts 23). And since God had told him, he believed it with all of his heart.

"For there stood by me this night an angel of the God to whom I belong and whom I serve, saying, 'Do not be afraid, Paul; you must be brought before Caesar; and indeed God has granted you all those who sail with you.' Therefore take heart, men, for I believe God that it will be just as it was told me" (Acts 27:23-25, NKJV).

I'm struck by how Paul's faith in God's ability to keep His promises, even in the face of a deadly storm, not only saved Paul, but also everyone else on the boat.

When we exercise faith, we may not always know just how many other lives will be touched and influenced by it; faith is contagious, and the Lord looks for those who will take Him at His Word, and strengthens them. And then, like with Abraham, He chooses to bless others through His faithful ones.

"For the eyes of the Lord run to and fro throughout the whole earth, to show Himself strong on behalf of those whose heart is loyal to Him…" (2 Chron. 16:9).

*–Louie D. Locke, senior pastor of Fountainhead Foursquare Church in Carson City, Nev.*

### Discussion Points:

1. What has God told you to do before your time is up or your ministry is concluded?

2. Is there anything, any circumstance that could sway you from fulfilling that assignment?

3. If you hold on and rely solely on God to help, how might the lives of others also be enriched by your obedience?

### Prayer Points:

▸ Fill me with contagious faith, especially in desperate circumstances.

▸ Encourage me by showing me when my faith in You impacts the lives of others.

▸ I want the kind of relationship with You, Lord, that results in lives being rescued and saved.

# ACTS 28

*"THIS IS FELLOWSHIP—MUTUAL ENCOURAGEMENT, BEING STRENGTHENED AND STRENGTHENING OTHERS IN RETURN—BASED FULLY ON THE COMMONALITY OF HAVING BEEN BROUGHT FROM DEATH TO LIFE, DARKNESS TO LIGHT, BY THE BLOOD OF JESUS CHRIST."*
**—LOUIE D. LOCKE**

# ACTS 28: BEWARE OF FANGS

BY SAM ROCKWELL

I don't think Luke the physician was trying to be funny. Nonetheless, I hear "rim-shots" after some of the verses in Acts 28.

For instance, in Acts 28:4, the residents of Malta viciously slander the apostle Paul: "No doubt," they hiss, "this man is a murderer!" (NKJV). A few verses later, in Acts 28:6, this same crowd breathlessly announces: "He is a god!"

The dark humor, of course, is that Paul is faced with the extremes of either accusation or adulation; he is either being aggressively denounced or openly flattered by the very same people!

This schizophrenic reaction, it seems to me, is a common experience of leaders who are leading in an optimal way. We should expect both sabotage and seduction.

My daughters, when they were still at home, were perfect examples of this. My eldest always tested her father as the saboteur. "No, Daddy," she would say, putting her foot down, "I won't!" In contrast, the younger one would typically attempt to butter me up: "Oh, Daddy," batting her eyes, "Really? Please?"

When we meet these responses to our leadership, it is usually not a sign that our followers are evil or fundamentally opposed to us; rather, they (and the Lord) are testing our character and resolve. As leaders, our best position is to be connected to followers while not being "fused" with them—to be differentiated, while not being disengaged.

Saboteurs and seducers tempt us to become reactive and defensive, but most respond positively when we are open, available to listen and patient, but always clear about the mission.

Let us pray this prayer: "Lord, help us to 'shake off the vipers' of our own insecurity and fear, and proceed confidently in the direction of

Your call, even if it leads us, as it did Paul, into the misunderstood territory of the dangerous unknown."

–*Sam Rockwell, Gateway District supervisor.*

### Discussion Points:

1. How do you typically respond when people you lead mount a surprise attack against you?

2. In light of this devotional, is it possible that people who lead such an assault are not your enemies? Is there some other, greater process in operation?

3. Discuss the significance of this statement for your ministry: "Saboteurs and seducers tempt us to become reactive and defensive, but most respond positively when we are open, available to listen and patient, but always clear about the mission."

### Prayer Points

- Guard my reactions, Lord, when others attack me.

- Keep me focused on the mission of the kingdom and not defensive toward people.

- Equip me to overcome my own insecurity and fear and instead follow Your call.

# ACTS 28: EMPOWERMENT THAT REACHES OUT

BY RON THIGPENN

I am awed by the scope of the tremendous journey chronicled in the book of Acts. From the promise of the Holy Spirit in chapter 1 through the birth of the church and the mighty "acts" of the apostles as they moved in the power of the Holy Spirit, we see the full breadth of God's calling for His people.

In this final chapter, we see Paul arriving in Rome more than three months after being shipwrecked on the island of Malta. He called together the local Jewish leaders and arranged a time to speak to the people about the gospel of Jesus Christ. As a result, "Some were persuaded by the things which were spoken, and some disbelieved" (Acts 28:24, NKJV).

Paul could have become discouraged by the hardness of hearts he encountered while on Malta. He could have lived out the rest of his days complacently, because he had already done enough, having endured persecution, prison, beatings and shipwreck for the sake of the gospel.

Instead, Paul continued to boldly share the gospel, even while under house arrest.

What can we learn from the book of Acts? We each have our own personal journey to walk in this life. God has empowered us by His Holy Spirit, not just for our own personal edification, but also so that we can fulfill the Great Commission. We are equipped by the Spirit to be people who demonstrate the love of God and His power to a dying world.

Acts 28 concludes by saying of Paul: "He welcomed all who visited him, boldly proclaiming the Kingdom of God and teaching about the Lord Jesus Christ. And no one tried to stop him" (vv. 30-31).

People or circumstances may try to stop us, but let's be His people who go forth, boldly proclaiming the kingdom of God and teaching about Jesus Christ. As we move into 2012, let's be the church God has called us to be. Let's "Reclaim Our Voice!"

*–Ron Thigpenn, Foursquare vice president and chief financial officer.*

### Discussion Points:

1. What will you take away from the book of Acts that will help you properly deal with people who oppose the gospel?

2. How important are your friends, family and ministry partners to the longevity and success of your ministry? How will you nurture those relationships so the gospel continues to go forth?

3. How will you encourage the fullness of the Holy Spirit in the lives of leaders you disciple?

### Prayer Points:

➤ Lord, I am grateful for the empowerment of Your Spirit in my life.

➤ Remind me to live in the power of Your Spirit for others and not only for myself.

➤ Encourage me to continue speaking clearly for You, Lord, especially when others try to silence me.

# ACTS 28: PUTTING MYSELF IN PAUL'S SHOES

BY LOUIE D. LOCKE

"And from there, when the brethren heard about us, they came to meet us as far as Appii Forum and Three Inns. When Paul saw them, he thanked God and took courage" (Acts 28:15, NKJV).

Paul was in Rome.

And the first thing he experienced there was a person meeting and greeting with fellow Christians who had traveled 50-60 miles to visit him.

Put yourself in Paul's shoes—in the previous years, he had experienced abandonment, rejection, constant persecution and wrongful accusations. He was treated like a criminal, had survived several assassination attempts and even recovered from a stoning. He'd been imprisoned in Jewish and Roman strongholds, had weathered the temperamental whims of Caesarean governor and had even lived through a shipwreck.

Then, upon arriving in Rome, he encountered brothers and sisters in Christ, a vivid reminder that he wouldn't be alone in this place. They were a flesh-and-blood fulfillment of God's promises and goodness to Paul. Their very presence caused him to give thanks to God, and also to be encouraged. He was filled to overflowing, and his time in Rome was characterized by his "preaching the kingdom of God and teaching the things which concern the Lord Jesus Christ with all confidence, no one forbidding him" (v.31).

This is fellowship—mutual encouragement, being strengthened and strengthening others in return—based fully on the commonality of having been brought from death to life, darkness to light, by the blood of Jesus Christ.

Years ago, I traveled to Birmingham, England, with a couple of friends in preparation for a mission trip. We didn't know a soul there but had heard that there was a Christian church that we could visit. We made our way there and found a small group of brothers and sisters meeting together for a meal and worship.

Though they'd never met us, they welcomed us to their table and into their midst with open arms. There was a tangible feeling that we were among family, and that we had something in common that bound us together in a way that only happens with the fellowship with other believers.

We talked, laughed, sang and prayed. They prayed for us, speaking words of knowledge, encouragement, hope and faith that touched our hearts to the very core. I can remember looking across the room through the candlelight at this gathering of believers, knowing that we were bound together in Christ, and that I knew I loved them and what's more, that they loved me.

A few days later, when we parted, I had the distinct sense that I wouldn't ever see any of these people again. But I also knew that when I did, here and in heaven, that we'd run to embrace each other and to celebrate the goodness and grace of our Lord Jesus Christ that sustains us from day to day.

–Louie D. Locke, senior pastor of Fountainhead Foursquare Church in Carson City, Nev.

**Discussion Points:**

1.  When compared to the latter years of Paul, have you ever met a Christian leader who has suffered as much hardship as Paul did?

2.  If you were in Paul's shoes, what feelings, thoughts, and emotions would you have dealt with during the events of Acts 28?

3.  Describe a relationship you have with another believer that is deep, spiritual, healthy and mutually fulfilling.

**Prayer Points:**

- Introduce me to other believers whose lives will enrich mine and whose partnerships will help establish the kingdom of God where I live and serve.

- Be the center of my relationships with others, Lord.

- Use me to share Your life and to encourage and strengthen people I meet and fellowship with.

# WRITING ACTS 29

BY TIM CLARK

The book of Acts has always read like a great adventure story to me. There's the explosive beginning, rich character development, surprising plot twists and epic journeys. And just when it seems the narrative should reach its crest, it continues to swell.

This book unfolds an infant faith that starts so small, all its Jewish adherents can fit into an upper room. But that eventually explodes into a phenomenon that encompasses countless multiethnic people spread all over the known world.

It's an addicting account. What makes it even better is that it's true—and that God is telling it. All of these miracles, all of this vibrant faith, all of those transformed lives—it's fantastic. When I finish chapter 28, I want to turn the page and find out what comes next.

So I turn the page, but the story is already over. If I were reading this for the first time, I would wonder if there was a misprint in my Bible; I'd think something must have been left out!

And even though I'm fully aware it will end, I still seem to be taken off guard. This brilliant story stops abruptly without a final climax or resolution. Paul is just hanging out in Rome under house arrest. End of story!

Or is it?

Many of us in the Foursquare family have been reading the whole book of Acts together every month this year, one chapter a day. As I write this, it's the 29th of the month, and already there is a gap in my daily pattern.

I want to read Acts 29. I want to find out what happens to Paul next. More than that, I want to see the continuation of the Spirit-filled proclamation of the gospel to even more of the world.

And then I remember what I learned way back in high school drama class. There are some plays and stories that suddenly end before we are ready for them to be done. It's a device that is used when the writer wants the audience or reader to feel the moral weight of what might come next.

The questions hang in the air: What would you do if you were these characters? How might God use you to spread this life-changing message?

Well, we are those characters. When a young church-planting network chose Acts 29 as their name, they got it exactly right. There is an Acts 29, and it is discovered among us.

We write Acts 29 when our lives are fueled by the high-octane life of the Spirit, and when we allow that reality to impact the world around us. We live Acts 29 when we single-mindedly function as citizens of another kingdom.

Ultimately, I believe the book of Acts is not as much a prescriptive model for church life as it is a descriptive account of what spontaneously happens to people and congregations when they are fully immersed in the Spirit.

People want to know the rest of the story. Let's live it and write it together.

*–Tim Clark, district supervisor of the Greater Los Angeles District. This article was adapted from his blog, www.pastortimclark.com. Used with permission.*

**Discussion Points:**

1. How will you ensure that the acts of the Holy Spirit continue today and in future generations?

2. How will you ensure that the people of God are constantly living in the power of the Spirit?

3. How will you ensure that the church of God continues to impact the world with His truth and life?

**Prayer Points:**

- My life is fully dedicated to Your purposes, Lord; Use me to continue the acts of the Holy Spirit today.

- Inspire me to share all that You have done for me, so that others will find eternal life too.

- Write an entirely new chapter full of miracles and new life, Lord, and do this in my life.

12355261R00132

Made in the USA
Charleston, SC
29 April 2012